RENU RECIPES

RENU RECIPES

Outstandingly Nutritious and Healthy Vegetarian Cuisine

Renu Sood

ANTHEM EDITIONS
www.anthempress.com

Anthem Editions
An imprint of Anthem Press
www.anthempress.com

This edition first published in UK and USA 2026
by ANTHEM EDITIONS
75–76 Blackfriars Road, London SE1 8HA, UK
or PO Box 9779, London SW19 7ZG, UK
and
244 Madison Ave #116, New York, NY 10016, USA

Copyright © Renu Sood 2026

The author asserts the moral right to be identified as the author of this work.

All rights reserved. Without limiting the rights under copyright reserved above, no part of this publication may be reproduced, stored or introduced into a retrieval system, or transmitted, in any form or by any means (electronic, mechanical, photocopying, recording or otherwise), without the prior written permission of both the copyright owner and the above publisher of this book.

British Library Cataloguing-in-Publication Data
A catalogue record for this book is available from the British Library.

Library of Congress Control Number: 2024947624

ISBN-13: 978-1-83999-378-7 (Pbk)
ISBN-10: 1-83999-378-2 (Pbk)

Photographer Oksana Merzlikina

This title is also available as an eBook.

ACKNOWLEDGEMENT

In preparing this cookbook, I have received wonderful encouragement and support from many quarters. I thank my sons – Fauji, Teji and Inu – and their wives for helping me decide on the specific dishes to include. The infectious enthusiasm of my grandchildren for my cooking has propelled me onward, to keep experimenting, learning and improving as a cook. My artist daughter-in-law, Natasha, and her teacher, Simone, were instrumental in crystallising the concept of this cookbook. I am extremely grateful to them. This cookbook would not be what it is without Oksana's exquisite photographs. Not only has she managed to capture perfectly the essence of the dishes, but she has always been available as a cherished advisor and companion. Finally, from the bottom of my heart I thank my husband and helpmate, Kamaljit. He was there at the very start of the project. He spurred me on and ensured I stayed the course. Without him, this cookbook would never have seen the light of day.

Renu Sood

CONTENTS

Preface — xi
Introduction — xiii

Breakfast & Brunch — 1
- Aloo/Potato Prantha — 2
- Gobi/Cauliflower Prantha — 4
- Egg Bhurji with Buttery Pranthas — 6
- Aloo Puri — 8
- Punjabi Puda — 10
- Healthy, Nutritious and Sugarless Milk Drink — 11

Lunch & Dinner — 13

Dals & Legumes — 15
- Kidney Beans/Rajma Curry — 16
- Dal Makhni/Sabut Urad — 18
- White Chole/Chickpeas — 20
- Black Chickpeas/Kala Chana Masala Curry — 22
- Moong Dal Tadka — 24
- Sabut Moong Dal — 25
- Dry Moong Dal — 26
- Dhuli Masoor Dal/Red Lentils — 27
- Sabut Masoor Dal — 28
- Arhar/Toor Dal — 30

Curries — 33
- Egg Potato Curry — 34
- Matar Paneer — 36
- Tofu Vegetable Curry with Coconut Milk — 38
- Lauki ki Sabji (Bottle Gourd Curry) — 40
- Sag Paneer — 42
- Shalgam ki Sabji (Turnip Curry) — 44

Vegetables — 47
- Baked Cauliflower with Cheese — 48
- Baked Parsnip and Spinach — 50
- Stir-fry Asparagus and Mushroom — 51
- Roasted Asparagus with Almonds, Capers and Dill — 52
- Stir-fry Tender Stem Broccoli with Garlic and Peanuts — 53
- Baked Aubergine Kachri with Onion — 54
- Steamed Brussels Sprouts — 55
- Stir-fry Cauliflower with Red Pepper and Chilli — 56
- Baked Crispy Thyme Potatoes — 57
- Baked Courgette with Cheese — 58
- Stir-fry Sweet Potato and Celery with Chilli — 59
- Stir-fry Broad Bean and Tofu — 60
- Stir-fry Aubergine, Long Mixed Colour Peppers, Potato and Onion — 61
- Steamed Cabbage and Broad Bean — 62
- Roasted Squash with Turmeric Chickpeas — 63
- Stir-fry Crispy Tofu and Blistered Snap Peas with Cashews — 64
- Paneer Subz Bahar — 66
- Baked Spinach and Cheese — 68
- Baked Swede and Leek — 69
- Bhindi Sabji (Okra Stir Fried) — 70
- Stir-fry Gajar (Carrot), Aloo (Potato) and Methi (Fenugreek Leaves) — 71

Baked Flat Beans	72
Stir-fry Parsnip and Leek	73
Aloo Palak (Potato Spinach)	74
Mixed Vegetable Bake	75
Aloo (Potato) Baingan (Aubergine) Sabji	76
Sag	78
Baingan Ka Bharta (Aubergine Mash)	80
Baked Butternut Squash	82

Salads — 83

Walnut and Tomato Salad with Pomegranate Molasses	84
Rocket Salad with Avocado and Cherry Tomatoes	85
Mango, Avocado, Pomegranate and Walnut Pieces	86
Baby Cucumbers and Lettuce	87
Beef Tomato with Spring Onion and Ginger Sauce	88
Egg, Avocado, Rocket Leaves with Pomegranate and Flaxseed Oil	89
Sugar Snap Peas with Feta, Dill and Yogurt	90
Grilled Beef Tomato with Chilli and Basil Leaves	91
Avocado, Cherry Tomatoes and Rocket Leaves	92
Sweet Potatoes, Chickpeas, Spinach and Pomegranate	93
Courgette and Herb Salad with Mozzarella and Dukkah	94
Sprouted Moong Dal	96
Avocado and Cucumber Salad with Fried Halloumi	98
Carrot, Mooli and Spring Onion with Capers	99
Mediterranean Chickpea Salad	100
Easy Greek Salad	101
Radicchio and Fruit Salad	102

Samphire, New Potatoes, Black Beans and Feta Cheese	103
Roasted Broccoli, Courgette and Chickpeas	104
Cauliflower, Butter Beans and Kale	105

Rice & Rice-Based — 107

Vegetable and Paneer Biryani	108
Jeera Rice	110
Plain Rice	111
Brown Rice	112
Matar Pulao	113
Red Rice	114

Chapatis — 117

Wheat Chapatis	118
Jowar (Sorghum) Roti (Chapati)	119

Chutneys & Raita — 121

Yogurt and Mint Chutney	122
Green Mango Chutney	123
Imli Ki Chutney or Tamarind Chutney	124
Seared Ginger Raita	125

Set Lunch & Dinner Menu — 127

Vegetable and Paneer Biryani	128
Pasta with Courgette and Mushroom	130
Potato, Courgette and Salad	132
Sweet Potato and Vegetable Tikki (Burger) with Sorghum	134
Rajma/Kidney Beans Curry and Jeera Rice	135

Snacks	**137**
Savoury Snacks	*139*
Aloo (Potato) Pakoras	140
Onion Pakoras	142
Aubergine Pakoras	144
Cauliflower Pakoras	146
Mixed Veg Pakora	148
Courgette Pakoras	150
Handwa	152
Besan Puda	153
Cheesy Crepes	154
Papdi Chaat	156
Healthy and Nutritious Roasted Makhana, Moong Phali, Sunflower and Pumpkin Seeds and Mixed Dry Fruit	158
Sweet Snacks	*161*
Flapjack	162
Almond Biscuits	163
Sweet & Salty Peanut Butter Roundies	164
Coconut Flour Cookies	166

Desserts	**167**
Paneer Dee Kheer	168
Chia Pudding	169
Rice Kheer from Malabar	170
Kada Prashad/Aate Ka Halwa	172
Gajar Da Halwa	174
Key Ingredients	**175**
How to Make Homemade Ghee	176
How to Make Homemade Yogurt	177
Indian Masala Chai (Spiced Milk Tea)	178
Indian Curry Masala	180
Grandchildren Favourites	**183**
Aloo Puri	184
Glazed Popcorn	186
Oat and Almond Pancakes	187
Porridge	188
Pasta with Fresh Tomato Sauce	189

PREFACE

Cookbooks are everywhere. The world's countless cuisines have their many cookbooks. Cookbooks have been written generation after generation, based on recipes passed down from grandmothers and mothers to their children and grandchildren. So, why another one? Why this one? My answers to these questions are what led me to this book. Perhaps the answers I gave may be of interest to you. Perhaps they will provide you with the key to understanding my approach to cooking – and even encourage you to try it out for yourself!

I was born and raised in Hindustan, in the north of India. I have always enjoyed cooking. How and what I cook is rooted in the place where I grew up. After marrying, my children arrived, and from their earliest days I nurtured them on the food of my homeland. Later on, my horizons widened to embrace the foods of the Mediterranean. These are the two great influences on my cooking today, a highly personal commingling of the cuisines of the North Indian and the Mediterranean worlds. Before and since this commingling, my children have always said that they love the food I give them. And now, their children – my grandchildren – say the same. Whenever I receive this praise, I get emotional, especially when the praise comes from my grandchildren. It is this love and praise that gave me the idea that my children, and their children, might like something more than just enjoying what I prepare for them; they might also like to learn about my cooking know-how and heritage. So, every week my grandchildren come round and I teach them by making rotis and a sabji or two together. But there is so much that I would like to share with them and never enough time. As this realisation dawned on me, the thought of a cookbook sprung to mind. Finally, I decided to take the plunge and devote myself to making a reality of it. The result of this is before you. What you see is a distillation of a lifetime's culinary experience. My hope is that this knowledge will be preserved by future generations of my family and enrich their lives. I also hope that it will enrich the lives of others who happen to chance across my cookbook.

There is a second reason without which this cookbook would have remained merely a thought. It is to do with my husband's type-2 diabetes. His view is that diabetes is not a disease as such but rather a particular state of being. A body in this state is defined by particular needs. To keep that body well, eating habits must be developed that correspond to those needs. I agree with this view. In living with diabetes, the body needs food with fewer potentially debilitating sugars. Over a period of years, my husband and I investigated various types of food. We eventually identified the kinds of ingredients required in practice to keep the blood sugar level below a workable maximum with only minor medication, all the while maintaining a relatively normal lifestyle. I am delighted (and relieved) to say that this approach has been a success. Because of the care with which I prepare the food for him, combined with his self-discipline over how much he eats, my husband, now in his mid-seventies, remains in good control of his blood sugar levels and is able to live more or less as he wishes.

These are the reasons behind my cookbook. I do not claim any great innovation for the recipes described. But I believe that they do have some novelty. In developing my recipes, I have experimented with many different ingredients. This is thanks to the enormous array of foods available in London from all corners of the world. It is also thanks to my husband, who has been a constant fount of inspiration and encouragement, introducing me to new types of flavours and aromas. These ingredients, far more varied and numerous than those available to me when I first started cooking, have allowed me to create new dishes or reimagine old ones. In doing so, I am as concerned with their taste as with their appearance. My experience over the decades has shown me again and again that both are equally important in producing dishes that family and friends happily tuck into with relish.

INTRODUCTION

This is my first cookbook. I have written it for everyone. It is for vegetarians and non-vegetarians alike. It is for those who wish to add new, delicious, attractive dishes to their culinary repertoire. It is for those interested in a traditional North Indian cuisine inflected with Mediterranean ingredients, flavours and techniques. Many of the recipes in this cookbook are quick to make and highly nutritious, addressing the imperatives of time in our all-too-busy lives and our deep-seated need for nourishing fare. But there is more. The recipes are designed to help keep blood sugar levels under control, particularly for those living with diabetes.

As this cookbook describes various types of dishes, I have grouped their recipes into several distinct categories. These are noted below. In the future, I intend to write more specialised cookbooks, dedicated to individual categories.

- Breakfast & Brunch
- Lunch & Dinner
  - Dals & Legumes
  - Curries
  - Vegetables
  - Salads
  - Rice & Rice-Based
  - Chapatis
  - Chutneys & Raita
  - Set Lunch & Dinner Menu
- Snacks
  - Savoury Snacks
  - Sweet Snacks
- Desserts
- Key Ingredients
- Grandchildren Favourites

You will see that the recipes end with my 'Grandchildren's Favourites'. This is because my grandchildren always have the last word on my cooking and it is for them above all that I have written this cookbook. They are eagerly waiting for it to appear so that they can have their own copy! My heartfelt wish is that these recipes are enjoyed by them – and everyone else who tries them – for many, many years to come.

BREAKFAST & BRUNCH

BREAKFAST & BRUNCH

ALOO/POTATO PRANTHA

Aloo prantha (also called paratha) is one of the popular Punjabi/North Indian breakfasts. It is stuffed with spicy potato filling and served with butter, alongside plain yogurt and pickle.

| Preparation time: 35 minutes | Cooking time: 15 minutes | Total time: 50 minutes | Makes: 8 pranthas |

Ingredients

For potato stuffing

3 or 4 medium potatoes, boiled and mashed
1 medium onion, cut into small pieces
1″ ginger, grated
2 green chillies, cut into small pieces (optional)
¼ tsp of flaked red chillies (optional)
Few sprigs of coriander, coarsely cut
1 tsp of amchoor (dry mango powder)
1 tbsp of dry methi (fenugreek)
½ tsp of ajwain (carom seeds)
1 tsp of rock salt or as per taste
Ghee or oil as required for roasting pranthas

For prantha dough

2 cups of whole wheat flour
½ tsp of rock salt
1 tbsp of ghee or oil
Water as required for kneading
Some extra flour for dusting/rolling

For serving

White or any butter
Plain yogurt
Mango or lemon pickle, as required

Method

Making potato filling

1. To make the potato filling, add all the ingredients of the filling to the mashed potatoes and mix them thoroughly. There should be no small pieces of potato left in it.
2. Add salt to taste and keep it aside.

Kneading dough

1. In another bowl, add flour, salt and ghee, and knead it with lukewarm water to make a smooth soft dough.
2. Cover and keep the dough aside for 20 to 30 minutes.

Breakfast & Brunch

Stuffing and rolling

1. Divide the dough into 8 pieces.
2. Take 1 small piece of dough and make a ball with your palm. Roll and flatten it with the use of dry flour into a circle of 5 to 5.5" in diameter.
3. Brush the flattened dough with little ghee or oil and place a handful of potato stuffing in the centre.
4. Take the edges and start pleating towards the centre.
5. Join the pleats together tightly without gaps to avoid the filling coming out.
6. In case any gaps are visible, take a small piece of dough or dry flour and cover the gap.
7. Press the pleats from the centre with the rolling pin, sprinkle some flour, flatten it and roll it to about the size of a chapati.
8. These should be flattened softly so that the filling does not come out.

Roasting

1. Heat the tava (skillet or griddle) on medium fire. When it gets hot, place the prantha on it. The temperature should be kept on medium to high as pranthas can harden if the heat is reduced.
2. When the side which is on the tava is partly cooked, flip it to the other side.
3. Spread some ghee on the partly cooked side.
4. Flip again and you will see brown spots on the prantha. Spread some ghee on this side also. A well-made and well-roasted aloo ka prantha will puff up.
5. Flip again once or twice until both the sides are cooked properly. Brown spots should be seen on both sides.
6. Prantha edges can be pressed with a spatula so that they are fried well. Sometimes, the edges are not cooked well.
7. Make all the pranthas like this and stack them up in a roti basket or casserole.
8. These are best enjoyed if they go directly from the tava to the serving plate, as by doing so, the crispness remains intact and it is loved by most.
9. Serve these with extra butter, yogurt and pickles of your liking.

Special Note

1. Ghee can be replaced with any oil to make it **vegan**.

BREAKFAST & BRUNCH

GOBI/CAULIFLOWER PRANTHA

Gobi prantha is one of the popular Punjabi/North Indian breakfasts. It is stuffed with spicy grated gobi filling and served with butter, alongside plain yogurt and pickle.

| Preparation time: 35 minutes | Cooking time: 15 minutes | Total time: 50 minutes | Makes: 8 pranthas |

Ingredients

For gobi stuffing

½ **gobi/cauliflower head if medium or 1 if small,** finely grated
1 **medium onion,** cut into small pieces
1″ **ginger,** grated
2 **green chillies,** cut into small pieces (optional)
¼ **tsp of flaked red chillies** (optional)
Few sprigs of coriander, coarsely cut
1 **tsp of amchoor (dry mango powder)**
1 **tbsp of dry methi (fenugreek)**
½ **tsp of ajwain (carom seeds)**
1 **tsp of rock salt** or as per taste
Ghee or oil as required for roasting pranthas

For prantha dough

2 **cups of whole wheat flour**
½ **tsp of rock salt**
1 **tbsp of ghee or oil**
Water as required for kneading
Some extra flour for dusting/rolling

For serving

White or any butter
Plain yogurt
Mango or lemon pickle, as preferred

Method

Making gobi filling

1. To make the gobi filling, add all the ingredients for the filling except salt to the grated gobi. Mix all the ingredients thoroughly.
2. Salt is added to each filling at the time of rolling the pranthas as the gobi can leave water if salt is added to the whole mixture in advance.

Kneading dough

1. In another big bowl, add flour, salt and ghee and knead it with lukewarm water to make a smooth, soft dough.
2. Cover and keep the dough for 20 to 30 minutes.

Stuffing and rolling

1. Divide the dough into 8 small pieces.
2. Take 1 piece and make a ball in your palm. Then flatten and roll the ball of dough with the use of dry flour to the size of 5 to 5.5" in diameter.
3. Take a small bowl, add a handful of gobi filling and a pinch of salt and mix it nicely.
4. Brush the flattened dough with little ghee or oil and place the salted gobi filling in the centre.
5. Take the edges and start pleating by bringing the pleats to the centre.
6. Join the pleats together. The pleats have to be joined well; otherwise, there will be gaps, and filling can come out.
7. In case any gaps are visible, take a small piece of dough and cover the gap.
8. Press the pleats from the centre with the rolling pin, sprinkle some flour and flatten this prantha to about the same size as a chapati.
9. These should be flattened softly, so that the gobi mixture does not come out.

Roasting

1. Keep the tava (skillet or griddle) on medium fire. When it gets hot, place the prantha on it. The temperature should be kept medium to high as pranthas can be hardened if the heat is reduced to low.
2. When the side which is on the tava is partly cooked, flip it to the other side.
3. Spread some ghee on the partly cooked side.
4. Flip again and you will see brown spots on it. Spread some ghee on this side also. A well-made and well-roasted prantha will puff up.
5. Flip again once or twice till both sides are cooked properly. Brown spots should be seen on both sides.
6. The edges can be pressed with a spatula so that they are fried well. Sometimes, the edges are not cooked well.
7. Make all the pranthas like this and stack them up in a roti basket or casserole.
8. These are best enjoyed if they go directly from the tava to the serving plate, as by doing this the crispness remains intact and it is loved by most.
9. Serve these with extra butter, yogurt and pickles of your liking.

Special Note

1. Ghee can be replaced with any oil to make it **vegan**.

BREAKFAST & BRUNCH

EGG BHURJI WITH BUTTERY PRANTHAS

Egg bhurji and prantha is one of the most popular Punjabi/North Indian breakfasts, which can also be used as brunch. It is eaten with extra butter and mango or lemon pickle.

| Preparation time: 15 minutes | Cooking time: 40 minutes | Total time: 55 minutes | Makes: 6 to 8 pranthas |

Ingredients

For prantha dough

300 g of whole wheat flour
3 tbsp of ghee or oil, 1 tbsp to be added to the flour when kneading, the rest to be used for rolling the pranthas
250 ml of lukewarm water or as required for kneading
Some extra flour for dusting/rolling
Ghee or oil required for roasting pranthas
1 tsp of rock salt
1 tsp of ajwain (carom seeds)

Egg bhurji

2 tbsp of butter
½ tsp of jeera (cumin seeds)
1 big onion, cut into small pieces
2 large vine tomatoes, cut into small pieces
8 eggs, lightly whisked
1 tsp of rock salt, more can be added as per taste
1 green chilli, cut into small pieces (optional)
¼ tsp of red chilli flakes (optional)
½ tsp of finely grated pepper
A bunch of coriander, chopped coarsely

For serving

White or any other type of butter
Mango or lemon pickle, as preferred

Method

Kneading dough

1. Take a medium-sized bowl. Add flour and ghee and knead it with water to make a smooth, soft dough.
2. Cover and keep the dough for a few minutes until the bhurji is being made. Dough can also be made 15 to 20 minutes earlier.

Egg bhurji

1. Take a frying pan and keep it on medium/high heat. Add butter, and as soon as it starts melting, add jeera.
2. As soon as it starts bubbling, add onion and stir it for 2 to 3 minutes. Add tomatoes and cover the pan until they are softened. This may take 7 to 8 minutes. The heat should be reduced to low. It should be stirred occasionally so that it does not get stuck to the base of the pan.
3. Add eggs, salt, green chilli and chilli flakes, and go on stirring until the eggs are completely done.
4. Add pepper and coriander and leave it covered.

Making pranthas

1. Dough can be divided into 6 or 8 pieces. The quantity depends on the size of the pranthas.
2. Take 1 piece of dough and make a ball in your palm. Roll out the dough with the rolling pin using dry flour. Flatten it to the size of 5 to 5.5″ in diameter.
3. Spread little ghee on the flattened dough, sprinkle a pinch of salt and a pinch of ajwain. Spread these nicely and then fold it into a square.
4. Flatten the square dough again to 5 to 6″ in size. This size can be made bigger if required.

Roasting pranthas

1. Keep the tava (skillet or griddle) on the fire. When it gets hot, place the prantha on it. The temperature should be kept medium to high as pranthas can harden if the heat is reduced to low.
2. When the side which is on the tava is partly cooked, flip it to the other side.
3. Spread some ghee on the partly cooked side.
4. Flip again and you will see brown spots on the prantha. Spread some ghee on this side as well. A well-made and well-roasted prantha will puff up.
5. Flip again once or twice till both sides are cooked properly. You should be able to see some brown colour in some places on both sides.
6. Prantha edges can be pressed with a spatula so that they are fried well. Sometimes, the edges are not cooked well.
7. Make all the pranthas like this and stack them up in a roti basket or casserole so that they remain warm until eaten.
8. The pranthas are best enjoyed if they go directly from the tava to the serving plate, as by doing this, the crispness remains intact, and it is loved by most.
9. Serve these with egg bhurji and enjoy.

Special Note

1. Ghee can be replaced by any oil to make it **vegan**.

BREAKFAST & BRUNCH

ALOO PURI

Aloo puri is a traditional Punjabi spiced potato curry served with puris. This is also one of the favourite dishes of our grandchildren.

| Preparation time: 25 minutes | Cooking time: 50 minutes | Total time: 75 minutes | Serves: 4 to 5 |

INGREDIENTS

FOR THE ALOO SABJI

350 g of potatoes or 5 medium-sized potatoes, boiled, peeled and diced, this sabji can also be made with raw potatoes
2 cups of water

MASALA OR TADKA

2 tbsp of ghee or any oil as per your choice
1 tsp of cumin seeds
1 pinch of asafoetida (hing)
½ tsp of black mustard seeds
4 cloves of garlic and 1½″ ginger, chopped in a food processor or cut into tiny pieces
¾ tsp of turmeric powder
1 tsp of coriander powder
1 tbsp of dry fenugreek leaves (methi)
1 tsp of rock salt, more can be added after tasting
½″ of lemon rind, nicely grated
1 tsp of lemon juice
2 tsp of tomato puree
½ a can of chopped tomatoes, approximately 250 g or 2 medium-sized tomatoes chopped in a food processor
1 green chilli, chopped or cut into small pieces (optional)
1 tsp of garam masala
Few sprigs of fresh coriander cut into small pieces, coarsely

METHOD

If raw potatoes are used, then a pressure cooker can be used. It will require 2 to 3 whistles or more until the potatoes are done.

1. Take a large heavy-bottom pan, keep on medium heat and add ghee or oil of your choice. When the ghee gets a little hot, add asafoetida, cumin and mustard seeds.
2. As soon as it starts bubbling, add the mixture of ginger and garlic and cook them for 1 to 2 minutes, stirring often.
3. Once the colour changes to light pink, add turmeric, coriander powder, fenugreek leaves and salt. After a couple of minutes, add lemon rind, lemon juice, tomato puree, chopped tomato and chilli and mix these nicely.
4. At this point, reduce the heat to low and cover the pan so that the tomatoes are combined properly and turn into a smooth paste. This takes 7 to 8 minutes. This paste should be stirred occasionally so that it does not get burnt.
5. Now add the potatoes and mix them nicely. Soon after, add water and mix it properly, bringing it to a boil.
6. Once it starts boiling, reduce the heat and let it simmer for 8 to 10 minutes.
7. While it is simmering, press a couple of potatoes with the spoon on the sides of the pan.
8. This is to get a slightly thicker consistency of the gravy. Starch from the potatoes also makes the gravy a little thick.
9. Once done, take it out in a serving bowl, sprinkle some garam masala and put the lid on to retain the aroma.
10. Sprinkle fresh coriander before serving.

Ingredients

For the puri

2½ to 3 cups of whole meal flour
1 tsp of oil
Lukewarm water to knead the flour – as required
Oil for frying

Method

1. Knead the flour into a stiff dough with water and oil. The dough for puris needs to be harder than for making chapatis. Once the dough is formed, drizzle with a dash of oil and use your fingers to cover the dough with it. Cover it and keep aside for about 30 minutes.
2. Make small balls of the dough according to your preferred size and shape them into balls. Dredge the working surface and the belan with a splash of oil.
3. Roll into rounds having 4 to 5 inches in diameter. You can roll 5 or more and keep these ready. Use oil instead of flour to roll out the puris as the dry flour will make the frying oil dirty.
4. Heat oil in a kadai or any deep pan at a high temperature. To check if the oil is ready for frying, drop a little piece the size of a pea into the oil and if it comes up immediately, the oil is ready.
5. Start adding puris slowly, 1 puri at a time, and flip each as it puffs up. This should be slightly pressed down with a stainless steel skimmer spatula.
6. When pressed, it puffs up a little. This should be turned over as soon as the colour changes to light brown. It will take only a few seconds.
7. Follow the same process until all the rolled puris are finished. Continue following the same process until the dough is finished.
8. Fry the puris at a high temperature in extra oil for the best, airy puris that don't absorb any extra oil.
9. Puris are ready when they are fully puffed up and are golden brown.
10. Remove and place these on paper napkins to remove excess oil.
11. Serve the puris with aloo sabji, along with sliced onions, some lemon wedges and some pickles.

Makes: 15 to 18 puris

Special Notes

1. Oil can be used to make the recipe **vegan**.
2. You can have the consistency of the aloo sabji as per your preference. However, avoid making it watery or thin. You can always add more water later if you feel the gravy has become too thick.
3. Special care is also taken that potatoes are not too mashed.

BREAKFAST & BRUNCH

PUNJABI PUDA

Punjabi puda is a sweet pancake made with whole wheat flour, fennel seeds and sugar. It can be had for breakfast along with besan ka puda or as a snack on its own.

| Preparation time: 10 minutes | Cooking time: 20 minutes | Total time: 30 minutes | Makes: 6 pudas |

Ingredients

120 g of whole wheat flour
1 tsp of fennel seeds
40 g of brown sugar or can be replaced with **jaggery**
200 ml of water plus a little more if required
Ghee for frying. **Oil** can be used to make it **vegan**

Method

1. Take a medium-sized bowl and add flour, fennel seeds and sugar and combine these nicely.
2. Slowly start adding water. Whisk it to make it in a smooth batter.
3. This batter should be like that of a pancake batter. This batter should be mixed well so that the sugar dissolves completely.
4. Take a flat pan and keep it on low/medium heat. I prefer a heavy-base steel pan/skillet.
5. Smear it lightly with ghee and spread 2 tbsp or a big scoop of batter onto the pan. The pan can also be picked up and moved around so that the batter spreads evenly.
6. Once the puda is nicely spread, the heat can be increased to medium.
7. Once the base of the puda has started cooking, you will see that the top has also started cooking. Flip the puda over and cook for approximately 2 minutes or until it seems nicely cooked. You can add a little ghee and flip again if it is not done. When you see that both sides change into little brown, it is cooked.
8. Take it out on a plate and go on making other pudas.
9. As a steel pan is used, it is advisable to use a steel spatula as the batter can easily stick to the base.
10. Serve these hot for the best taste and texture. Enjoy with a hot cup of tea.

Special Notes

1. It is important to keep the heat on low when spreading the puda onto the pan; otherwise, it can easily burn.
2. Once it is flipped, heat can be increased to medium.
3. You can increase or decrease the sugar as per your preference.
4. Oil can be used to make it **vegan**.
5. Instead of sugar, try using isomaltulose, a natural alternative to sugar that contains far fewer calories than sugar and thus can have great benefits for those concerned about blood sugar levels. Moreover, the glycemic index (GI) of isomaltulose is much less than it is for sugar.

BREAKFAST & BRUNCH

HEALTHY, NUTRITIOUS AND SUGARLESS MILK DRINK

Healthy, nutritious and sugarless milk drink is a nutritious, healthy and tasty drink. This can be enjoyed with breakfast on its own or added to oats or any other cereal of your choice.

| Preparation time: 5 minutes | Cooking time: 10 minutes | Total time: 15 minutes | Serves: 1 |

Ingredients

- **1 cup of milk;** any type of milk can be used as per your preference
- **1 tbsp of mixed seeds – sunflower and pumpkin** (equal quantities of both seeds mixed and stored in an airtight glass bottle)
- **½ tsp of chia seeds**
- **½ tsp of ground flaxseeds**
- **½ tsp of coconut flakes**
- **1 tbsp of mixed berries – raisins, cranberries and goji berries** (equal quantities of 3 berries mixed and stored in an airtight glass bottle)
- **½ tsp of plant-based pea protein** (optional)

Method

1. Take a pan. Add 1 cup of milk and keep it on medium heat.
2. Add all the above ingredients and bring it to a boil.
3. As soon as it starts boiling, bring it to a simmer and stir it a couple of times with a spoon.
4. Leave it to simmer for 10 minutes.
5. Ready to drink now.
6. Pour it in the cup.

Special Note

1. Any other milk, such as soya, almond or oat milk, can be used to make it **vegan**.

LUNCH & DINNER

DALS & LEGUMES

DALS & LEGUMES

KIDNEY BEANS/RAJMA CURRY

| Preparation time: 15 minutes | Cooking time: 60 minutes | Total time: 75 minutes | Serves: 4 to 6 |

INGREDIENTS

TO PRESSURE-COOK

1½ cups raw kidney beans, soaked in 4 to 5 cups of lukewarm water. If preferred, raw beans can be replaced with **2 red kidney beans tins 400 g each**
3½ cups of water, approximately 28 oz
1 tbsp of ghee or oil of your choice
1 tsp of rock salt

MASALA OR TADKA

¼ tsp hing powder
2 tbsp of ghee or oil of your choice
½ tsp of ginger powder
1 large onion, 4 cloves of garlic and 1½" ginger, chopped in a food processor or cut into tiny pieces
1 green chilli, chopped or cut into small pieces (optional)
½" of lemon rind, nicely grated
2 tsp of tomato puree
½ a can of chopped tomatoes, approximately 250 g or 3 medium-sized tomatoes chopped in a food processor
1 tbsp of dry fenugreek leaves (methi)
½ tsp of turmeric powder
1 tsp of cumin seeds
½ tsp of black mustard seeds
1 tsp of coriander powder
1 tsp of rock salt, more can be added after tasting
1 tsp of garam masala
Few sprigs of fresh coriander, cut into small pieces, coarsely

METHOD

1. Wash the beans at least 3 times and then soak them overnight in approximately 4 to 5 cups of lukewarm water. The water should be enough so that the beans are nicely soaked overnight. In the morning, drain the water in which the beans were soaked, then transfer to a pressure cooker. Add water, salt and ghee.
2. Place the pressure cooker on high heat for 4 whistles. Let the pressure release naturally. Beans should be completely soft at this point.
3. Take a large heavy-bottomed pan and keep on medium heat and add ghee or oil of your choice. When the ghee gets a little hot, add hing, cumin and mustard seeds. As soon as they start bubbling, add the mixture of onion, ginger and garlic and cook these for 5 to 6 minutes, stirring often. Once the colour changes to light pink, add turmeric, salt, ginger powder, coriander powder and fenugreek leaves. Then add chopped tomato, tomato puree and chili, and mix these nicely. At this point, reduce the heat to low and cover the pan so that the tomatoes are combined properly and turn into a smooth paste. This takes 7 to 8 minutes. This paste should be stirred occasionally so that it does not get burned.
4. Add the boiled beans along with the water in which they were boiled. Mix them properly and let it simmer for 20 to 30 minutes. While they are simmering, take 1 or 2 scoops of beans out from the pan and mash them with a potato masher, then mix these again with the rest of the bean curry. This makes the curry creamier and thickens it.

DALS & LEGUMES

5. If the consistency seems quite thick, a few tablespoons of water can be added as per your preference.
6. Half of the coriander leaves should be added while the curry is still simmering.
7. Finally, switch off the heat and sprinkle garam masala, and cover it so that the flavour is retained.
8. Sprinkle fresh coriander before serving.

Special Notes

1. Serve with plain or jeera rice and enjoy.
2. Oil can be used to make the recipe **vegan**.

DALS & LEGUMES

DAL MAKHNI/SABUT URAD

Preparation time: 10 minutes   Cooking time: 50 minutes   Total time: 60 minutes   Serves: 6

Ingredients

To pressure-cook

¾ cup of sabut urad dal
¼ cup of rajma (red kidney beans) 60 g
1 tsp of rock salt
1 tbsp of ghee, can be replaced with any type of oil of your choice to make it **vegan**
1" **ginger,** cut into thin pieces
2 cloves of garlic, cut into thin pieces
1 green chilli, whole (optional)
3½ cups of water or 28 oz, more can be added depending on the consistency required

Masala or tadka

2 tbsp of ghee or any oil of your choice
½ tsp of hing powder
1 tsp of cumin seeds
½ tsp of mustard seeds
1 medium onion, cut into tiny pieces
1" **ginger,** cut into small pieces
2 cloves of garlic, cut into small pieces
½ tsp of red chilli flakes (optional)
200 g of chopped tomato
1 tsp of tomato puree
½ tsp of garam masala
Few sprigs of coriander, cut coarsely
2 tbsp of single cream for garnish

Method

1. Wash and rinse urad dal and rajma in a large bowl. Dal and rajma should be rinsed 3 to 4 times. Soak them in enough water and leave them overnight.
2. In the morning, drain the water in which dal and rajma were soaked. Transfer these to a pressure cooker and add water, salt, ghee, ginger, garlic and whole chilli.
3. Pressure-cook on high-medium heat for at least 4 whistles. Let the pressure release naturally. At this point, the dal and rajma should be completely cooked. You should be able to mash them with your fingers.
4. At this point, remove the weight of the cooker and let the dal simmer on low heat for at least 20 to 25 minutes. This should be occasionally stirred to avoid sticking to the bottom.
5. A little more water can be added if dal seems too thick.
6. While the dal is put to simmer, tadka should be made. To make tadka, add ghee or oil in a medium-sized pan. As soon as it becomes a little hot, add cumin and mustard seeds and hing powder. As soon as it starts bubbling, add onion, ginger and garlic and cook these for 5 to 6 minutes or until they have turned into light pink. Add chopped tomato and tomato puree and chilli and mix these nicely.
7. At this point, reduce the heat to low and cover the pan so that the tomatoes are combined properly and turn into a smooth paste. Leave this covered for another 5 minutes. This paste should be stirred occasionally so that it does not get burned.

DALS & LEGUMES

8. Add the masala to the dal, mix it completely and leave it on low heat for another 20 minutes to simmer. By this time, the dal should have become creamy.
9. More salt can be added as per the taste.
10. Add garam masala and garnish the dal makhni with cream and coriander leaves.

Special Note

1. Serve with plain rice, jeera rice or chapatis and enjoy.

DALS & LEGUMES

WHITE CHOLE/CHICKPEAS

Preparation time: 15 minutes Cooking time: 45 minutes Total time: 60 minutes Serves: 4 to 6

Ingredients

To pressure-cook

1½ cups of chickpeas
1 tsp of rock salt
1 tbsp of ghee or any oil of your choice
3½ cups water

Masala or tadka

2 tbsp of ghee or any oil of your choice
½ tsp of hing powder
1 tsp of jeera (cumin seeds)
1 bay leaf
½ tsp of mustard seeds
2 cloves
2 brown cardamom
1 tbsp of dry fenugreek leaves (methi)
1 medium onion, 1″ ginger and 3 cloves of garlic, chopped in a food processor or cut into tiny pieces
¾ tsp of turmeric powder
1 tsp of coriander powder
250 g of chopped tomato, 3 medium-sized fresh tomatoes chopped in a food processor
1 tsp of tomato puree
½″ of unwaxed lemon rind, nicely grated
1 green chilli, chopped or cut into tiny pieces (optional)
½ tsp of red chilli flakes (optional)
1 tbsp of lemon juice
½ tsp of garam masala
Few sprigs of coriander, cut coarsely

Method

1. Place chole in a large pot and rinse 3 times. Add enough water, cover it and leave it overnight to soak.
2. In the morning, drain the water in which chickpeas were soaked. Transfer them to a pressure cooker and add fresh water, salt and ghee.
3. Keep the pressure cooker on high-medium heat for at least 4 whistles. Let the pressure release naturally. At this point, the chickpeas should be completely cooked. You should be able to mash them with your fingers.

Masala or tadka

1. To make tadka, add ghee or oil in a medium-sized pan. As soon as it becomes a little hot, add cumin and mustard seeds and hing powder. As soon as it starts bubbling, add bay leaf, cloves, cardamom, fenugreek leaves and stir for 1 minute, then add onion mixture. Let it cook for 5 to 6 minutes or until it has turned light pink. Add chopped tomato, tomato puree, lemon rind, green chilli and chilli flakes, and mix these nicely.
2. At this point, reduce the heat to low and cover the pan so that the tomatoes are combined properly and it turns into a smooth paste. Leave this covered for another 7 to 8 minutes. This paste should be stirred occasionally so that it does not get burned.
3. Add the masala to the chole. By this time, the chole should be completely soft. If the curry seems watery, some of the chickpeas should be taken out, mashed and added again. This will make the curry thicker.

DALS & LEGUMES

4. After adding the masala, the curry should be kept on the heat for another 10 to 15 minutes to simmer.
5. More salt can be added as per the taste.
6. Add garam masala and garnish with coriander leaves.

SPECIAL NOTES

1. Serve with plain rice, jeera rice or chapatis and enjoy.
2. Oil can be used to make the recipe **vegan**.
3. This dish is one of the favourite dishes of children.

DALS & LEGUMES

BLACK CHICKPEAS/KALA CHANA MASALA CURRY

| Preparation time: 15 minutes | Cooking time: 45 minutes | Total time: 60 minutes | Serves: 4 to 6 |

Ingredients

To pressure-cook

1½ cups of dried black chickpeas (400g cooked chickpeas)
1 tsp of rock salt
1 tbsp of ghee or any oil of your choice
3½ of cups water

Masala or tadka

2 tbsp of ghee or any oil of your choice
½ tsp of hing powder
1 tsp of jeera (cumin seeds)
1 bay leaf
½ tsp of black or brown rye (mustard seeds)
2 brown cardamom
1 tbsp of dry fenugreek leaves (methi)
1 medium onion, 1″ ginger and 3 cloves of garlic, chopped in a food processor or cut into tiny pieces
¾ tsp of turmeric powder
1 tsp of coriander powder
250 g of chopped tomatoes or 3 medium-sized fresh tomatoes, chopped in food processor
1 tsp of tomato puree
½″ of unwaxed lemon rind, nicely grated
1 green chilli, chopped or cut into tiny pieces (optional)
½ tsp of red chilli flakes (optional)
1 tbsp of lemon juice
½ tsp of garam masala
Few sprigs of coriander, cut coarsely

Method

1. Place the chana in a large pot and rinse them 3 times. Add enough water, cover it and leave it overnight to soak.
2. In the morning, drain the water in which these were soaked. Add fresh water and transfer them to a pressure cooker. Add salt and ghee.
3. Keep the pressure cooker on high-medium heat for at least 4 whistles. Let the pressure release naturally. At this point, the chana should be completely cooked. You should be able to mash them with your fingers.

Masala or tadka

1. To make tadka, add ghee or oil to a medium-sized pan. As soon as it becomes a little hot, add hing powder, cumin and mustard seeds. When it starts bubbling, add cloves, bay leaf, cardamom, fenugreek leaves and stir for 1 minute, then add onion mixture. Reduce the heat and let it cook for 5 to 6 minutes or until it has turned light pink. Add chopped tomato, tomato puree, lemon rind, green chilli and chilli flakes, and mix these nicely.
2. Cover the pan so that the tomatoes are combined properly and turn into a smooth paste. Leave this covered for another 7 to 8 minutes. This paste should be stirred occasionally so that it does not get burned.
3. Add the tadka to the chana. If the curry seems watery, some of the chana should be taken out, mashed and added to the curry again. This will make the curry thicker.

4. After adding the masala, the curry should be kept on the heat for another 10 minutes to simmer.
5. Add lemon juice. More salt can be added as per the taste.
6. Add garam masala and garnish with coriander leaves.

Special Notes

1. Serve with plain rice, jeera rice or chapatis and enjoy.
2. Oil can be used to make the recipe **vegan**.
3. This dish is one of the favourite dishes of children.

DALS & LEGUMES

MOONG DAL TADKA

| Preparation time: 20 minutes | Cooking time: 15 minutes | Total time: 35 minutes | Serves: 4 to 6 |

Ingredients

To pressure-cook

1 **cup of moong dhuli.** It is also known as split petite yellow lentils
3 **cups of water**
¾ **tsp of rock salt,** more can be added as per taste
½ **tsp of haldi/turmeric**
1 **tbsp of ghee, can be replaced with any type of oil of your choice** to make it **vegan**
1 **small onion, 1″ ginger, 2 cloves of garlic,** cut into thin pieces
1 **medium-sized tomato,** cut into small pieces
2 **cloves of garlic,** cut into thin pieces
1 **green or red chilli,** cut into small pieces (optional)

Masala or tadka for dal

1 **tbsp of ghee or any oil of your choice**
1 **tsp of cumin seeds**
½ **tsp of mustard seeds**
1 **tsp of tomato puree**
½ **tsp of garam masala**
Few sprigs of coriander, cut coarsely

Method

1. Wash and rinse dal. Dal should be rinsed 3 to 4 times.
2. Add dal, water, salt, haldi, ghee, onion, ginger, garlic and tomato to the pressure cooker.
3. Put the pressure cooker on high heat and cook for only 1 whistle. Let it release naturally.
4. In the meantime, start preparing tadka.
5. To make tadka, add ghee to a pan. As soon as it becomes a little hot, add cumin and mustard seeds. As soon as they start bubbling, add tomato puree and stir for 2 to 3 minutes, then add to the dal.
6. Add garam masala and garnish with coriander leaves.

Special Note

1. Serve with plain rice, jeera rice or chapatis and enjoy.

DALS & LEGUMES

SABUT MOONG DAL

| Preparation time: 10 minutes | Cooking time: 25 minutes | Total time: 35 minutes | Serves: 5 to 6 |

INGREDIENTS

TO PRESSURE-COOK

1 cup of sabut moong dal
1 tsp of rock salt
¾ tsp of turmeric powder
1 tbsp of ghee
1 medium onion, cut into small pieces
1 medium-sized fresh tomato, cut into small pieces, **or 200 g of chopped canned tomato** can also be used
1″ ginger, cut into thin pieces
2 cloves of garlic, cut into thin pieces
1 green chilli, cut into small rounds (optional)
3 cups of water or approximately 28 oz, more can be added depending on the consistency required

MASALA OR TADKA FOR DAL

2 tbsp of ghee or any oil of your choice
1 tsp of cumin seeds
½ tsp of mustard seeds
½ tsp of red chilli flakes (optional)
1 tsp of tomato puree
½ tsp of garam masala
Few sprigs of coriander, cut coarsely

METHOD

1. Wash and rinse dal in a large bowl. Dal should be rinsed 3 to 4 times. Soak in 4 cups of water overnight.
2. In the morning, drain the water in which dal was soaked. Transfer these to a pressure cooker and add salt, turmeric powder, ghee, onion, tomato, ginger, garlic, chilli and water.

3. Pressure-cook on high-medium heat for at least 3 whistles. Let the pressure release naturally. At this point, dal should have been nearly cooked.
4. At this point, remove the weight of the cooker and let it simmer on low heat for at least 8 to 10 minutes. It should be occasionally stirred to avoid sticking to the bottom.
5. A little more water can be added if dal seems too thick.
6. While the dal is put to simmer, tadka should be made. To make tadka, add ghee or oil to a medium-sized pan. As soon as it becomes a little hot, add cumin and mustard seeds. As soon as it starts bubbling, add tomato puree and chilli flakes and cook for 1 to 2 minutes until they have mixed completely.
7. Mix these with dal and mix it completely, then leave it on low heat for another 2 to 3 minutes to simmer. By this time, the dal should have become creamy.
8. More salt can be added as per the taste.
9. Add garam masala and garnish with coriander leaves.

SPECIAL NOTES

1. Serve with plain rice, jeera rice or chapatis and enjoy.
2. Oil can be used to make the recipe **vegan**.

DALS & LEGUMES

DRY MOONG DAL

Preparation time: 20 minutes   Cooking time: 15 minutes   Total time: 35 minutes   Serves: 6

Ingredients

To pressure-cook

1 cup of moong dhuli. It is also known as split petite yellow lentils
¼ cup of water
¾ tsp of rock salt, more can be added as per taste
¼ tsp of haldi (turmeric)
1 tbsp of ghee, can be replaced with any type of oil of your choice to make it **vegan**

Masala or tadka for dal

1 tbsp of ghee or any oil of your choice
1 tsp of cumin seeds
½ tsp of mustard seeds
1 small onion, 1″ ginger, 3 cloves of garlic, cut into thin pieces
1 medium-sized tomato, cut into small pieces
1 tsp of tomato puree
1 green or red chilli, cut into small pieces (optional)
½ tsp of garam masala
Few sprigs of coriander, cut coarsely

Method

1. Wash and rinse the dal. Dal should be rinsed 3 to 4 times.
2. Add dal, water, ghee, salt and haldi to the pressure cooker.
3. Put the pressure cooker on high heat and cook for only 2 whistles. Let it release naturally.
4. In the meantime, start preparing tadka. To make tadka, add ghee in a pan. As soon as it becomes a little hot, add cumin and mustard seeds. As soon as it starts bubbling, add the mixture of onion, ginger and garlic. Stir for a couple of minutes, then add tomato and stir for another 2 to 3 minutes. Add tomato puree and chilli to the tomato mixture. Go on stirring for another minute.
5. Add this to the dal and combine the mixture completely with the dal, but a great care should be taken when mixing as the dal should not be mashed.
6. Sprinkle garam masala on the top and leave it covered so that the aroma is retained.
7. Garnish with coriander leaves before serving.

Special Note

1. Serve with plain rice, jeera rice or chapatis and enjoy.

DALS & LEGUMES

DHULI MASOOR DAL/RED LENTILS

| Preparation time: 10 minutes | Cooking time: 25 minutes | Total time: 35 minutes | Serves: 4 to 6 |

Ingredients

To pressure-cook

1 cup of masoor dal
300 ml of water
¾ tsp of rock salt, more can be added as per taste
½ tsp haldi (turmeric)
1 tbsp of ghee or any oil of your choice
1 small onion, 1″ ginger, 2 cloves of garlic, cut into thin pieces
1 medium-sized tomato, cut into small pieces
1 green or red chilli, cut into small pieces (optional)

Masala or tadka

1 tbsp of ghee or any oil of your choice
1 tsp of cumin seeds
½ tsp of mustard seeds
1 tsp of tomato puree
½ tsp of garam masala
Few sprigs of coriander, cut coarsely

Method

1. Wash and rinse dal. Dal should be rinsed 3 to 4 times.
2. Add dal, water and all other ingredients in the pressure cooker.
3. Put the pressure cooker on high heat and cook for only 1 whistle. Let it release naturally.
4. In the meantime, start preparing the tadka. Keep a pan on medium heat. Add ghee. As soon as it becomes a little hot, add cumin and mustard seeds. As soon as it starts bubbling, add tomato puree and stir for 2 to 3 minutes. Then mix it with the dal.
5. Add garam masala and garnish with coriander leaves.

Special Notes

1. Serve with plain rice, jeera rice or chapatis and enjoy.
2. Oil can be used to make the recipe **vegan**.

DALS & LEGUMES

SABUT MASOOR DAL

| Preparation time: 10 minutes | Cooking time: 25 minutes | Total time: 35 minutes | Serves: 5 to 6 |

Ingredients

To pressure-cook

1 cup of sabut masoor
1 tsp of rock salt
¾ tsp of turmeric powder
1 tbsp of ghee
1 medium onion, cut into small pieces
1 medium-sized fresh tomato, cut into small pieces, **or** 200 g of chopped canned tomato can also be used
1" ginger, cut into thin pieces
2 cloves of garlic, cut into thin pieces
1 green chilli, cut into small rounds (optional)
3 cups of water or approximately 28 oz, more can be added depending on the consistency required

Masala or tadka for dal

2 tbsp of ghee or any oil of your choice
1 tsp of cumin seeds
½ tsp of mustard seeds
½ tsp of red chilli flakes (optional)
1 tsp of tomato puree
½ tsp of garam masala
A few sprigs of coriander, cut coarsely

Method

1. Wash and rinse the dal in a large bowl. The dal should be rinsed 3 to 4 times.
2. Transfer this to a pressure cooker and add salt, turmeric powder, ghee, onion, tomato, ginger, garlic, chilli and water.
3. Pressure-cook on high-medium heat for at least 2 whistles. Let the pressure release naturally. At this point, the dal should be nearly cooked.
4. At this point, remove the weight of the cooker and let it simmer on low heat for at least 8 to 10 minutes. It should be occasionally stirred to avoid sticking to the bottom.
5. A little more water can be added if dal seems too thick.
6. While the dal is put to simmer, the tadka should be made.

To make tadka

1. Add ghee or oil to a small pan. As soon as it becomes a little hot, add cumin and mustard seeds. As soon as it starts bubbling, add tomato puree and chilli flakes and cook for 1 to 2 minutes until they have mixed completely.
7. Mix these with dal, and mix it completely, and leave it on low heat for another 2 to 3 minutes to simmer. By this time, the dal should have become creamy.
8. More salt can be added as per the taste.
9. Add garam masala and garnish with coriander leaves.

Special Notes

1. Serve with plain rice, jeera rice or chapatis, and enjoy.
2. Oil can be used to make the recipe **vegan**.

DALS & LEGUMES

DALS & LEGUMES

ARHAR/TOOR DAL

| Preparation time: 10 minutes | Cooking time: 35 minutes | Total time: 45 minutes | Serves: 4 to 5 |

Ingredients

2 tbsp of ghee or oil or butter
¼ tsp of hing (asafoetida)
¾ tsp of cumin seeds
½ tsp of mustard seeds
Few curry patta leaves
1 medium-sized onion, 1″ ginger, 2 cloves of garlic, cut into thin pieces or finely chopped
½ tsp of haldi (turmeric)
2 medium-sized tomatoes, cut into small pieces, or half a can of chopped tomatoes (approximately 200 ml)
1 tsp of tomato puree
½ tsp of lemon rind if unwaxed lemon is used (optional)
2 medium-sized carrots, grated
¾ to 1 tsp of pink Himalayan salt; any salt can be used
1 cup of arhar dal
2½ cups of water
1 green or red chilli, cut into small pieces (optional)
¼ tsp of red flake chillies (optional)
1 tbsp of kasuri methi, crushed
1 tbsp of lemon juice
½ tsp of garam masala (optional)
Few sprigs of fresh coriander leaves, cut coarsely

Method

1. Wash and rinse the dal. Dal should be rinsed 3 to 4 times. Keep aside.
2. Add ghee to a pressure cooker. As soon as it melts, add hing, cumin seeds and mustard seeds. As soon as they start to splutter, add curry leaves.
3. Soon after, add the mixture of onion, garlic and ginger and go on stirring until it becomes pink. Then add haldi.
4. Then add tomatoes, tomato puree, lemon rind and salt and mix these nicely and let it cook for 5 to 7 minutes or until all the tomatoes become soft and it becomes like a smooth paste.
5. Add carrots, both the chillies and mix it nicely and soon after add the washed dal and mix these again. Go on mixing for a minute. Then add water and close the pressure cooker.
6. It may require 2 or 3 whistles to be ready. You should check after 2 whistles, and if dal is not yet soft enough and smooth, give it another whistle.
7. Let the pressure cooker release itself. If the consistency looks fine, then add kasuri methi crushed in your palm and lemon juice, and let it boil for another 8 to 10 minutes.
8. More water can be added if required.
9. Add more salt if required.
10. Take out the dal in a serving dish, sprinkle garam masala and cover the dish so that the aroma can be retained.
11. Garnish with coriander leaves before serving.

Special Notes

1. Arhar dal is mainly enjoyed with plain rice or jeera rice. Chapatis or pranthas can also be eaten with it.
2. Oil can be used to make the recipe **vegan**.
3. This dish is one of the favourites of children.

DALS & LEGUMES

CURRIES

CURRIES

EGG POTATO CURRY

| Preparation time: 15 minutes | Cooking time: 45 minutes | Total time: 60 minutes | Serves: 4 to 6 |

Ingredients

2 boiled potatoes, cut into 6 to 8 pieces depending on the size
6 hard-boiled eggs

Masala or tadka

2 tbsp of ghee or any oil as per your choice
1 tsp of cumin seeds
½ tsp of black mustard seeds
3 cardamom pods (optional)
2 small cinnamon sticks (optional)
1 tbsp of dry fenugreek leaves (methi)
1 large onion, 4 cloves of garlic and 1½" ginger, chopped in a food processor or cut into tiny pieces
1 green chilli, chopped or cut into small pieces (optional)
½" lemon rind, nicely grated
½ tsp of turmeric powder
1 tsp of coriander powder
2 tsp of tomato puree
½ can of chopped tomatoes, approximately 250 g or **3 medium-sized tomatoes** chopped in a food processor
1 tsp of rock salt, more can be added after tasting
1 tsp of garam masala (optional)
Few sprigs of fresh coriander, cut into small pieces, coarsely
1 tsp of corn flour (optional) if the onion paste seems watery or **1 tsp of sesame seeds**

Method

1. To make this mouth-watering spicy egg curry, keep a pan of cold water on high heat and add the eggs for boiling. Add some salt to it to avoid them from breaking. When it starts boiling, bring the heat to medium and ensure that it keeps on boiling. Boil them for 6 minutes and set them aside.

2. Take a large heavy-bottom pan, keep on medium heat and add ghee or oil of your choice. When the ghee gets a little hot, add cumin seeds, mustard seeds, cardamom pods and cinnamon sticks. As soon as it starts bubbling, add the mixture of onion, ginger and garlic and cook these for 5 to 6 minutes stirring often. Once the colour changes to light pink, add turmeric, salt, coriander powder and fenugreek leaves. Then add chopped tomato, tomato puree and chilli, and mix these nicely. At this point, reduce the heat to low and cover the pan so that the tomatoes are combined properly and turn into a smooth paste. This takes 8 to 10 minutes. This paste should be stirred occasionally so that it does not get burned.

3. The consistency of the paste should be like yogurt. Add potatoes and mix them properly for 1 minute. Add 1 cup of water and let it cook, stirring occasionally until the mixture thickens. The sauce should be runny. If the sauce isn't runny, add a few tablespoons of water.

4. In case the mixture seems watery, mix the cornflour in 3 to 4 spoons of cold water and add to the sauce. Instead of cornflour, 1 tsp of sesame seeds can be added to thicken the mixture. I use sesame seeds. If any of these ingredients are used, keep it simmering for another 5 minutes.

5. Half of the coriander leaves should be added while the curry is still simmering. The sauce should be left to

simmer for another 10 minutes. Sprinkle garam masala and cover it for a couple of minutes so that the flavour is retained.

6. Add all but 2 eggs and stir gently. Heat until the eggs are warmed through. Halve the remaining eggs lengthwise and arrange on top, yolk-side up. Finally, switch off the heat and sprinkle fresh coriander before serving.

Special Notes

1. Serve with plain rice, jeera rice or chapatis and enjoy.
2. Oil can be used to make the recipe **vegan**.

CURRIES

MATAR PANEER

Preparation time: 10 minutes | Cooking time: 25 minutes | Total time: 35 minutes | Serves: 4

Ingredients

250 g of paneer, cut into 3 cm cubes
150 g of frozen peas, defrosted
1 large onion, 4 cloves of garlic and 1½″ ginger, chopped in a food processor or cut into tiny pieces
1 green chilli, chopped or cut into small pieces (optional)
2 tbsp of ghee or any oil as per your choice
½″ of unwaxed lemon rind, nicely grated
2 tsp of tomato puree
½ a can of chopped tomatoes, approximately 250 g or 3 medium-sized tomatoes, chopped in a food processor
1 tbsp of dry fenugreek leaves (methi)
¾ tsp of turmeric powder
1 tsp of cumin seeds
½ tsp of black mustard seeds
1 tsp of coriander powder
2 bay leaves
3 cardamom pods (optional)
2 small cinnamon sticks (optional)
2 tbsp of plain yogurt
1 cup of water, a little more can be added if required
1 tsp of rock salt, more can be added after tasting
1 tsp of garam masala
Few sprigs of fresh coriander, cut into small pieces, coarsely
1 tsp of corn flour (optional) if the onion paste seems watery or **1 tsp of sesame seeds** can be added

Method

1. Before you start with the recipe, soak the paneer pieces in hot water for 20 minutes.
2. Take a large heavy-bottom pan and keep it on medium heat and add ghee or oil of your choice. When the ghee gets a little hot, add cumin, mustard seeds, cardamom pods and cinnamon sticks. As soon as it starts bubbling, add the mixture of onion, ginger and garlic and cook these for 7 to 8 minutes stirring often. Once the colour changes to light brown, add turmeric, salt, coriander powder and fenugreek leaves. Then add chopped tomato, tomato puree, chilli and yogurt and mix them nicely. At this point, reduce the heat to low and cover the pan so that the tomatoes are combined properly, and it turns into a smooth paste. This paste should be stirred occasionally so that it does not get burned.
3. The consistency of the paste should be like yogurt. Add paneer and peas and mix them properly for 1 to 2 minutes. Add water and let it boil. As soon as it starts boiling, reduce the heat and let it simmer for 6 to 7 minutes stirring occasionally.
4. In case the mixture seems watery, mix the cornflour in 3 to 4 spoons of cold water and add it to the sauce. Instead of cornflour, 1 tsp of sesame seeds can be added to thicken the mixture. I use sesame seeds.
5. Half of the coriander leaves should be added while the curry is still simmering.

CURRIES

6. Add garam masala and cover it for a couple of minutes so that the flavour is retained.
7. Sprinkle fresh coriander before serving.

SPECIAL NOTES

1. Serve with plain rice, jeera rice or chapatis and enjoy.
2. Oil can be used to make the recipe **vegan**.

CURRIES
TOFU VEGETABLE CURRY WITH COCONUT MILK

| Preparation time: 20 minutes | Cooking time: 20 minutes | Total time: 40 minutes | Serves: 4 to 6 |

Ingredients

225 g of tofu, cut into 1″ pieces
2 carrots, cut into small cubes
1 big potato, cut into small cubes
½ **cup of frozen peas**
200 ml of coconut milk

Masala or tadka

2 tbsp of ghee or any oil as per your choice
1 tsp of cumin seeds
½ **tsp of black mustard seeds**
1 large onion, 4 cloves of garlic and 1½″ ginger, chopped in a food processor or cut into tiny pieces
1 green chilli, chopped or cut into small pieces (optional)
1 tbsp of dry fenugreek leaves (methi)
¾ **tsp of turmeric powder**
1 tsp of coriander powder
1 tsp of rock salt, more can be added after tasting
½″ **lemon rind,** finely grated
2 tsp of tomato puree
½ **a can of chopped tomatoes, approximately 250 g** or **3 medium-sized tomatoes,** chopped in a food processor
½ **cup of water**
1 tsp of garam masala
Few sprigs of fresh coriander, cut into small pieces, coarsely

Method

1. This curry is one of our grandkids' favourite dishes.
2. Take a pressure cooker and keep it on medium heat. Add ghee or the oil of your choice. When the ghee gets a little hot, add cumin and mustard seeds. As soon as they start bubbling, add the mixture of onion, ginger and garlic and cook these for 7 to 8 minutes stirring often. Once the colour changes to light pink, add turmeric, salt, coriander powder and fenugreek leaves. After a minute, add chopped tomatoes, tomato puree and chilli, and mix these nicely. At this point, reduce the heat to low and cover the pan so that the tomatoes are combined properly and turn into a smooth paste. Leave it covered for another 5 minutes. The paste should be stirred occasionally so that it does not get burned.
3. The consistency of the paste should be like yogurt. Add carrots, potatoes and peas and mix these for 1 minute. Add tofu pieces and mix again so that all the tofu and vegetables are nicely covered with the paste. Add half a cup of water and mix once again.
4. Cover the pressure cooker and give 2 whistles. When the pressure is released, add coconut milk and half of the coriander leaves, and let it simmer for another 5 minutes.
5. Move the curry to a bowl and add garam masala, and cover it so that the flavour is retained.
6. Sprinkle fresh coriander before serving.

Special Notes

1. Serve with plain rice, jeera rice or chapatis and enjoy.
2. Oil can be used to make the recipe **vegan**.

CURRIES

CURRIES
LAUKI KI SABJI (BOTTLE GOURD CURRY)

| Preparation time: 10 minutes | Cooking time: 15 minutes | Total time: 25 minutes | Serves: 4 to 6 |

Ingredients

1 medium-sized lauki, peeled and chopped into ½" pieces
1 large onion, 3 cloves of garlic and 1" ginger, chopped in a food processor or cut into tiny pieces
1 green chilli, chopped or cut into small pieces (optional)
2 tbsp of ghee or any oil as per your choice
½" unwaxed lemon rind, nicely grated
2 fresh tomatoes, chopped in a food processor or cut into small pieces, **or ½ a can of chopped tomatoes** can also be used
1 tsp of tomato puree (optional)
1 tbsp of dry methi (fenugreek leaves)
1 tsp of jeera (cumin seeds)
½ tsp of black rye (mustard seeds)
½ tsp of haldi (turmeric powder)
1 tsp of dhania (coriander powder)
1 tsp of rock salt, more can be added after tasting
1 tsp of lemon juice
1 tsp of garam masala
Few sprigs of fresh dhania (coriander leaves), cut into small pieces, coarsely
¼ cup of water or more can be added if you want it to be more watery

Method

1. Keep the pressure cooker on medium heat and add ghee or oil of your choice. When the ghee gets a little hot, add cumin and mustard seeds. As soon as it starts bubbling, add the mixture of onion, ginger and garlic and cook these for 5 to 7 minutes stirring often. Once the colour changes to light brown, add haldi, salt, dhania powder and methi leaves. Soon after, add chopped tomato, tomato puree and chilli and mix these nicely. At this point, reduce the heat to low and cover the pan so that the tomatoes are combined properly and turn into a smooth paste. This takes another 5 to 7 minutes. This paste should be stirred occasionally so that it does not get burned.
2. Add lauki and combine with the sauce. Add water and give 2 whistles or keep it for 5 minutes after the pressure has built up.
3. Sometimes, lauki pieces remain hard even after 2 whistles. If this happens, another whistle can be given.
4. Add lemon juice and take it out in a bowl. Sprinkle garam masala and cover it.
5. Before serving, decorate it with dhania leaves.

Special Notes

1. Lauki sabji is ready. Serve with chapatis, prantha and rice and enjoy.
2. Oil can be used to make the recipe **vegan**.

CURRIES

CURRIES

SAG PANEER

| Preparation time: 10 minutes | Cooking time: 35 minutes | Total time: 45 minutes | Serves: 4 to 6 |

Ingredients

450 g of paneer, cut into 3 cm cubes and soaked in hot water for 20 to 30 minutes in advance
750 g of frozen fresh spinach
1 tbsp of besan (gram flour)
2 to 3 tbsp of water

Masala or tadka

2 tbsp of ghee or any oil as per your choice
1 tsp of cumin seeds
½ tsp of black mustard seeds
1 large onion, 4 cloves of garlic and 1½″ ginger, chopped in a food processor or cut into tiny pieces
1 green chilli, chopped or cut into small pieces (optional)
¾ tsp of turmeric powder
1 tsp of rock salt, more can be added after tasting
½″ of unwaxed lemon rind, nicely grated
2 tsp of tomato puree
½ a can of chopped tomatoes, approximately 250 g or **3 medium-sized tomatoes,** chopped in a food processor
1 tsp of garam masala

Method

1. Take a medium heavy-based pan and keep on medium heat. Add spinach.
2. Mix besan and water and make it a thin paste and add to the spinach. Once it reaches the boiling stage, reduce the heat, cover the pan and let it simmer for 15 minutes, stirring occasionally so that it does not stick to the base. By this time, no water should be visible.
3. Take another pan and keep it on medium heat, then add ghee or oil of your choice. When the ghee gets a little hot, add cumin and mustard seeds. As soon as they start bubbling, add the mixture of onion, ginger and garlic and cook these for 5 to 6 minutes stirring often. Once the colour changes to light pink, add turmeric and salt. Then add chopped tomato, tomato puree, chilli, lemon pieces and mix these nicely. At this point, reduce the heat to low and cover the pan so that the tomatoes combine properly and turn into a smooth paste. This paste should be stirred occasionally so that it does not get burned.
4. The consistency of the paste should be like yogurt. Take out paneer pieces from the water, add them to the tadka and stir occasionally for 2 to 3 minutes.
5. Add spinach to this mixture and combine these thoroughly. Keep the heat low, cover the pan and let it cook for another 8 to 10 minutes, stirring occasionally.
6. Add garam masala and cover it for a couple of minutes to retain the flavour.

Special Notes

1. Serve with plain rice, jeera rice or chapatis and enjoy.
2. Oil can be used to make the recipe **vegan**.

CURRIES

CURRIES
SHALGAM KI SABJI (TURNIP CURRY)

| Preparation time: 10 minutes | Cooking time: 20 minutes | Total time: 30 minutes | Serves: 4 to 6 |

INGREDIENTS

FOR STEAMING

600 g of turnip, cut into cubes
Enough water to add to the steamer

MASALA OR TADKA

2 tbsp of ghee or any oil as per your choice
1 tsp of jeera (cumin seeds)
½ tsp of black rye (mustard seeds)
1 tbsp of dry methi (fenugreek leaves)
½ tsp of haldi (turmeric powder)
1 tsp of dhania (coriander powder)
1 tsp of rock salt, more can be added after tasting
1 large onion, 3 cloves of garlic and 1″ ginger, chopped in a food processor or cut into tiny pieces
1 green chilli, cut into small pieces (optional)
½″ unwaxed lemon rind, nicely grated
2 fresh tomatoes, chopped in a food processor or cut into small pieces or ½ **a can of 400 g chopped tomatoes**
1 tsp of tomato puree (optional)
1 tsp of lemon juice
½ tsp of garam masala
Few sprigs of fresh dhania (coriander leaves), cut into small pieces or chopped coarsely
¼ cup of water or more can be added if you want it to be more watery

METHOD

1. Add water to the lower part of the steamer and keep it on high heat. As soon as it starts boiling, reduce the heat to medium and let it simmer for 10 minutes or until the pieces have become soft.
2. While turnips are being steamed, keep a heavy-based frying pan on medium heat and add ghee or oil of your choice. When the ghee gets a little hot, add cumin and mustard seeds. As soon as they start bubbling, add the mixture of onion, ginger and garlic and cook these for 5 to 7 minutes stirring occasionally. Once the colour changes to light pink, add haldi, salt, dhania powder and methi leaves. Soon after, add chopped tomato, tomato puree and chilli, and mix these nicely. At this point, reduce the heat to low and cover the pan to allow the tomatoes to combine properly and turn into a smooth masala. This takes another 5 to 7 minutes. The masala should be stirred occasionally so that it does not get burnt.
3. Add steamed turnip pieces and combine with the sauce and cover the pan. Keep it on the heat for another 5 minutes. Add lemon juice. It should be stirred occasionally to avoid it sticking to the base.
4. Transfer it to a bowl, sprinkle garam masala and cover it.
5. Before serving, decorate it with dhania leaves.

SPECIAL NOTES

1. Shalgum ki sabji is best served with chapatis, prantha and rice.
2. Oil can be used to make the recipe **vegan**.

CURRIES

VEGETABLES

VEGETABLES

BAKED CAULIFLOWER WITH CHEESE

| Preparation time: 30 minutes | Cooking time: 40 minutes | Total time: 70 minutes | Serves: 4 |

Ingredients

1 medium-sized cauliflower, broken into 2" florets
½ broccoli, broken into 2" florets

Masala or tadka

2 to 3 tbsp of sunflower oil or ghee, as required
1 tsp of cumin seeds
½ tsp of black mustard seeds
1 large onion, 4 cloves of garlic and 1½" ginger, chopped in a food processor or cut into small pieces
1 green chilli, chopped or cut into small pieces (optional)
Few small pieces of unwaxed lemon rinds
2 tsp of tomato puree
½ a can of 400 g chopped tomatoes or 2 medium-sized tomatoes cut into small pieces
1 tsp of turmeric powder
1 tsp of coriander powder
1¼ tsp of rock salt, more can be added after tasting
150 g of grated mature cheddar cheese. Any other hard cheese can also be used
Few sprigs of fresh coriander, cut into small pieces, coarsely
½ tsp of garam masala (optional)
1 tbsp of corn flour, optional, only to be used if the onion mixture seems watery

Method

1. Place the steamer with water on high heat. As soon as the water starts boiling, add cauliflower and broccoli pieces to the top pan and let them boil. As soon as it starts to boiling, reduce the heat to the lowest. Leave it for 8 to 10 minutes or until these are tender. Check 1 piece, and if it has become tender, remove them from the heat and spread the pieces on a tray to dry. Keep the water aside.
2. Take a large heavy-based pan and keep on medium heat, then add oil. When the oil gets a little hot, add cumin and mustard seeds. As soon as they start bubbling, add the mixture of onion, ginger and garlic. When it turns light pink, add turmeric, salt and coriander powder. After 2 to 3 minutes, add chopped tomato, tomato puree and chilli and mix these nicely. At this point, reduce the heat to low and cover the pan to allow the tomatoes to combine properly and turn into a smooth paste. This takes 5 to 7 minutes.
3. Check occasionally so that it does not get burnt. At this point, add the water to the paste. Boil it for 5 minutes more or until the mixture becomes like yogurt so that it can stick to the cauliflower pieces. If the liquid seems thick, add more water. Boil it for a couple of minutes.
4. If the paste looks watery, a corn flour mixture can be made by mixing 1 tbsp of corn flour with 3 to 4 tsp of water. Add this to the paste to make the sauce less watery. However, if the liquid is not watery, there's no need to add corn flour. If corn flour is added, bring the mixture to a boil, let it simmer for a couple of minutes, then set it aside. Finally, add lemon juice and garam masala.
5. Preheat the grill to 220°C. Take a large oven dish and transfer the cauliflower pieces into the dish, and pour masala over them. The florets and masala should be

nicely combined so that each piece is covered with the masala, but special care should be taken to ensure that these do not break.

6. Grated cheese should be spread over these, and the dish should be moved to the preheated grill. It should be set for 8 to 10 minutes or until the cheese has melted and begins to brown.
7. Fresh sprigs of coriander can be sprinkled over the dish before serving.

Special Note

1. The masala should be tasted when it is mixed with cauliflower to check if the salt is fine. If required, some more can be added.

VEGETABLES

BAKED PARSNIP AND SPINACH

| Preparation time: 10 minutes | Cooking time: 30 minutes | Total time: 40 minutes | Serves: 4 |

Ingredients

1 pound of parsnip, cut into small cubes
200 g of leaf spinach, washed and towel-dried
½ tsp of turmeric powder
1 tsp of rock salt, more can be added to taste
¼ tsp of black pepper, finely ground
2 tbsp of extra virgin olive oil

Method

Before mixing the spinach with parsnip, add a pinch of salt, but it should be added just before it is ready to be mixed.

1. Preheat the oven to 200°C. I use an electric oven which has a fan option.
2. Add parsnip pieces to the large shallow dish. Add haldi, salt, pepper and olive oil and toss thoroughly. Parsnip pieces should be spread evenly in the dish. Roast the parsnip pieces until they are tender. This may take 20 minutes.
3. Remove it from the oven and keep it on the table top.
4. Add spinach leaves that are already prepared to the dish and toss and turn them completely. After mixing, place it again in the oven for another 10 minutes. After 10 minutes, the dish will be ready.

Menu suggestion: This can be served with fish, thin-cut baked potatoes prepared at the same time in the oven, and salad.

VEGETABLES

STIR-FRY ASPARAGUS AND MUSHROOM

| Preparation time: 12 minutes | Cooking time: 8 minutes | Total time: 20 minutes | Serves: 4 |

Ingredients

2 tbsp of extra virgin olive oil
1 tsp of cumin seeds
½ tsp of mustard seeds
4 cloves of garlic, cut into small pieces
¼ tsp of turmeric powder
1 pound of mushrooms, washed, thinly sliced and spread on the paper towel
300 g of asparagus, cut into 3″ pieces
½ tsp of fine rock salt, more can be added after tasting
¼ tsp of ground black pepper
¼ tsp of red chilli flakes (optional)
Few sprigs of fresh coriander, coarsely cut, for decoration

Method

1. Take a pan with a heavy base and keep it on medium heat. Add oil and wait until the oil heats up. Add cumin seeds and mustard seeds, and as soon as it starts bubbling, add garlic pieces. The heat should be reduced to low, and as soon as the colour of the garlic changes to pink, add turmeric and salt. Soon after, add mushroom and asparagus.
2. These should be nicely mixed and stirred continuously for a minute. At this point, the heat should be changed to high. Cover the pan for a couple of minutes. By then, the asparagus and mushrooms should have softened. In case there is little water, the pan should be uncovered and left on high heat for a couple of minutes or until the water has evaporated.
3. Once the water has evaporated, pepper should be added. Before serving, coriander pieces should be sprinkled over the dish.

Menu suggestion: This can be served as a side dish with fish, potatoes and salad.

VEGETABLES

ROASTED ASPARAGUS WITH ALMONDS, CAPERS AND DILL

| Preparation time: 10 minutes | Cooking time: 15 minutes | Total time: 25 minutes | Serves: 4 |

Ingredients

600 g of asparagus, woody ends trimmed
3 tbsp of olive oil
½ tsp of rock salt
¼ tsp of black pepper
25 g of unsalted butter
25 g of flaked almonds
30 g of baby capers or regular, pat-dried on kitchen paper
10 g of dill, roughly chopped

Method

1. Use a preheated oven at 200°C.
2. Mix the asparagus with 1 tbsp of oil, salt and pepper. Arrange on a large parchment-lined baking tray, spaced well apart and roast for 8 to 12 minutes until the asparagus is soft and starting to brown in some places. Transfer to a large serving plate and set aside.
3. Add butter to a small saucepan and place it on a medium heat. Once melted, add the almonds and fry for 1 to 2 minutes, stirring frequently, until the almonds are golden brown. Pour the almonds and butter evenly over the asparagus.
4. Using the same saucepan, add the remaining 2 tbsp of oil on high heat. Once hot, add the capers and fry for 1 to 2 minutes, stirring continuously until they have opened up and become crisp. Using a slotted spoon, remove the capers from the oil and sprinkle over the asparagus, along with the dill. Discard the oil and serve warm.

VEGETABLES
STIR-FRY TENDER STEM BROCCOLI WITH GARLIC AND PEANUTS

| Preparation time: 15 minutes | Cooking time: 10 minutes | Total time: 25 minutes | Serves: 4 |

Ingredients

500 g of tender stem broccoli, cut into 4″ pieces and cut in half if thick
3 tbsp of extra virgin olive oil
3 cloves of garlic, finely sliced
3 cm piece of ginger, peeled and thinly sliced
1 orange, 4 strips of finely shaved skin
40 g of salted roasted peanuts, roughly chopped
½ tsp of rock salt
¼ tsp of finely ground pepper

Method

1. Take a heavy-based saucepan and keep it on a medium heat. When it is a little hot, add half of the olive oil to it and at the same time, add garlic, ginger, orange strips and peanuts and fry for 2 to 3 minutes stirring frequently, until the peanuts and garlic turn light pink. Transfer them to a small bowl to stop them from cooking and set aside.
2. Take a steamer and add water. As soon as the water starts boiling, add broccoli pieces to the top pan and let them boil for 4 to 5 minutes until cooked. Transfer the cooked broccoli to a serving plate and set aside.
3. Keep the same saucepan on medium fire which was used for the peanuts. Add the remaining oil. As soon as vapour starts appearing, add the broccoli pieces and stir continuously for a minute, turning softly. Add salt and pepper and transfer to a serving plate. Sprinkle the mixture of peanuts on top. The dish is ready to be eaten.
4. This can be served as a side.

VEGETABLES

BAKED AUBERGINE KACHRI WITH ONION

Preparation time: 15   Cooking time: 20 minutes   Total time: 35 minutes   Serves: 4

Ingredients

2 aubergines, cut into small round pieces
2 big onions, cut into thin, long pieces
½ **tsp of turmeric powder**
1 tsp of fine rock salt, more can be added as per taste
½ **tsp of black pepper,** finely ground
⅓ **tsp of dry basil or oregano herb**
¼ **tsp of flaked chilli** (optional)
3 to 4 tbsp of extra virgin olive oil

Method

1. Heat the oven to 220°C. I use the oven with a fan option, and it works well. Take a large shallow baking dish and add aubergine and onion pieces. Add turmeric, salt, pepper, herbs, chilli powder (if using) and oil and mix these nicely. The dish will come out good if all the pieces are nicely spread in the tray and put in the oven.
2. Keep the dish in the oven for 20 minutes. Before taking it out, it is important to check if the aubergine pieces have become soft and have turned a little bit brown and crispy.

Menu suggestion: This dish can be served with fish, thin-cut baked potatoes baked at the same time in the oven, along with some salad.

VEGETABLES

STEAMED BRUSSELS SPROUTS

| Preparation time: 10 minutes | Cooking time: 15 minutes | Total time: 25 minutes | Serves: 4 |

Ingredients

500 g of Brussels sprouts, trimmed and peeled
2 tbsp of olive oil
1 tsp of cumin seeds
½ tsp of mustard seeds
2″ of ginger, grated
4 cloves of garlic, cut into long thin pieces
½ tsp of turmeric powder
1 tsp of rock salt
½ tsp of flaked red chilli (optional)
¼ tsp of black pepper, finely ground

Method

1. Take a steamer with water and keep on high heat. As soon as the water starts boiling, add Brussels sprouts on the top pan and let it boil for 8 to 10 minutes or until the sprouts have become soft to touch. Once the sprouts have been added to the pan, the heat can be reduced to medium.
2. Take a heavy-based pan and keep on medium heat. When it gets a little hot, add oil and leave it for a while and add cumin and mustard seeds. As soon as they start bubbling, add ginger and garlic, and leave it on the heat until it turns slightly pink. Then, add turmeric powder and mix everything well.
3. After a couple of minutes, add Brussels sprouts and salt and mix it properly. Reduce the heat to low, cover the pan, let it cook for 5 minutes. After 5 minutes, stir gently to avoid breaking the sprouts. Add chilli powder and pepper and mix well to ensure the sprouts are evenly coated.

Vegetables

STIR-FRY CAULIFLOWER WITH RED PEPPER AND CHILLI

Preparation time: 10 minutes Cooking time: 20 minutes Total time: 30 minutes Serves: 4

Ingredients

500 g of cauliflower, washed with salted water, cut into 1″ pieces
2 tbsp of coconut oil
1 tsp of cumin seeds
½ tsp of mustard seeds
¾ tsp of turmeric powder
2″ ginger, peeled and grated
4 cloves of garlic, cut into long thin pieces
1 tsp of rock salt, more can be added to taste
1 big red pepper, cut into small strips
½ tsp of flaked red chilli (optional)
¼ tsp of black pepper, finely ground
3 to 4 tbsp of leftover steamed water
Few sprigs of fresh coriander

Method

1. Take a steamer with water and keep on high heat. As soon as the water starts boiling, add cauliflower pieces on the top pan and let it boil for 6 to 8 minutes or until the pieces have become soft to touch. Once these are added to the pan, the heat can be reduced to medium. The water from the steamer should be kept aside.
2. Take a heavy-based pan and keep on medium heat. When it gets a little hot, add oil and leave it for a while and add cumin and mustard seeds. As soon as it starts bubbling, add the ginger and garlic, and cook until they turn slightly pink. Then add turmeric powder and mix everything well.
3. After a couple of minutes, add cauliflower pieces, pepper pieces, salt and chilli (if used) and mix them properly. Heat should be reduced to low and the pan should be covered and left for 5 minutes. If the mixture sticks to the pan, add a few spoons of steamed water. After 5 minutes, it should be stirred slowly so that it does not break. Add pepper and mix again to ensure everything is properly coated with the vegetables.
4. Leave it for a minute so that the pepper can become a little soft but still a little crunchy.
5. Garnish with coriander leaves.

Special Note

1. Pepper pieces can also be boiled together with cauliflower or added at the time of stir-frying. If added at the time of stir-frying, these will keep a crunchy texture.

VEGETABLES

BAKED CRISPY THYME POTATOES

Preparation time: 5 minutes   Cooking time: 20 minutes   Total time: 25 minutes   Serves: 4

Ingredients

600 g or 6 red medium-sized potatoes, thinly sliced
50 g of melted butter
1 tsp of rock salt, more can be added as per taste
¾ tsp of black pepper, finely ground
2 tbsp of thyme, only leaves
Few sprigs of thyme for decoration

Method

1. Preheat the oven to 220°C. I use the oven with a fan option, and it works well. Take a large shallow dish and add potatoes, butter, salt, pepper and thyme leaves.
2. Combine these nicely and keep in the preheated oven. Potatoes will come out crispy if all the pieces are nicely spread out.
3. Keep it in the oven for 20 minutes. Before taking it out, it is important to check if the potato pieces have softened, turned brownish and crispy.
4. Garnish with sprigs of thyme.

Menu suggestion: This dish can be served with fish or any vegetable and salad.

VEGETABLES

BAKED COURGETTE WITH CHEESE

| Preparation time: 10 minutes | Cooking time: 25 minutes | Total time: 35 minutes | Serves: 4 |

Ingredients

3 courgettes, cut into small round pieces
1 big onion, cut into thin long pieces
¼ tsp of turmeric powder
¾ tsp of fine rock salt, more can be added as per taste
½ tsp of black pepper, finely ground
⅓ tsp of dry basil or oregano herb
¼ tsp of flaked red chilli (optional)
3 to 4 tbsp of extra virgin oil
120 g of mozzarella cheese, grated

Method

1. Preheat the oven to 220°C. I use the oven with a fan option, and it works well. Take a large shallow baking dish and add courgette and onion pieces. Add turmeric, salt, pepper, herbs, chilli powder (if using) and oil and mix these nicely. The dish will come out good if all the pieces are evenly spread out before putting it in the oven.
2. Keep in the oven for 20 minutes. Before taking them out, it is important to check if the courgette pieces have softened and turned brownish. Spread the cheese evenly and put the dish back in the oven on high heat under the grill for 5 minutes or until the cheese has turned a light brownish colour.

Menu suggestion: This dish can be served as a side with fish, along with thin-cut baked potatoes cooked in the oven at the same time, and a side of salad.

VEGETABLES

STIR-FRY SWEET POTATO AND CELERY WITH CHILLI

Preparation time: 10 minutes   Cooking time: 20 minutes   Total time: 30 minutes   Serves: 4

Ingredients

2 tbsp of ghee or coconut oil
1 tsp of cumin seeds
½ tsp of mustard seeds
2″ ginger, peeled and grated
4 cloves of garlic, cut into long thin pieces
1 green chilli, cut into small pieces (optional)
¾ tsp of turmeric powder
1 tsp of rock salt, more can be added as per taste
500 g or 2 big sweet potatoes, boiled
4 sprigs of celery, cut into small pieces
¼ tsp of black pepper, finely ground
Few sprigs of fresh coriander, cut coarsely

Method

1. Take a heavy-based pan and keep on medium heat. When it gets a little hot, add ghee and leave it for a while before adding cumin and mustard seeds. As soon as it starts bubbling, add ginger, garlic and chilli if used. Stir for a minute or until it turns a little pink, then add turmeric powder and mix these properly.
2. After a couple of minutes, add celery and stir it nicely, then cover for 2 to 3 minutes. Add sweet potato and salt, mix properly and cover it for 5 minutes. The heat should be reduced to low. Stir it and cover again. After 5 minutes, the dish should be ready. It is important to check if the sweet potatoes and celery pieces have become soft.
3. This should be transferred to a bowl and garnished with black pepper and coriander leaves.

VEGETABLES

STIR-FRY BROAD BEAN AND TOFU

| Preparation time: 10 minutes | Cooking time: 15 minutes | Total time: 25 minutes | Serves: 4 |

Ingredients

3 tbsp of extra virgin olive oil
1 tsp of cumin seeds
½ tsp of black rai
4 cloves of garlic, peeled and cut into small pieces
1″ ginger, grated
¾ tsp of turmeric powder
¾ tsp of rock salt, more can be added to taste
350 g of broad beans, frozen and defrosted
400 g of firm tofu, drained and cut into small cubes
¼ tsp of black pepper, finely ground
¼ tsp of red chilli flakes (optional)
Few sprigs of coriander, coarsely cut

Method

1. Take a heavy-based frying pan and keep it on medium heat. Add 2 tbsp of oil, and as soon as it gets a little hot, add cumin and mustard. As soon as it starts bubbling, add garlic and ginger. When the garlic pieces turn light pink, add turmeric and salt and stir nicely. Add broad beans, mix it well with the mixture and cover the pan. The heat should be reduced to low and cook for 7 to 8 minutes or until soft. Remove it from the pan and keep it aside.

2. Use the same pan. Keep it on medium fire and add the remaining oil and as soon as it gets hot, add tofu pieces along with a little salt and keep stirring it occasionally until they turn a little brown. Mix in the broad beans and leave it on the heat for another 5 minutes.

3. Remove from heat. Add black pepper and mix it well. Garnish with coriander leaves.

VEGETABLES

STIR-FRY AUBERGINE, LONG MIXED COLOUR PEPPERS, POTATO AND ONION

Preparation time: 15 minutes | Cooking time: 20 minutes | Total time: 35 minutes | Serves: 4

Ingredients

3 tbsp of extra virgin olive oil
1 tsp of cumin seeds
½ tsp of mustard seeds
1 red onion, cut thinly lengthwise
3 cloves of garlic, thinly cut lengthwise
1½″ ginger, peeled and thinly sliced **(approximately 20 g)**
3 strips of unwaxed lemon rind, cut into small pieces
½ tsp of turmeric
1 small green chilli, cut into small pieces (optional)
1 tsp of rock salt, more can be added to taste
2 long purple aubergine, cut lengthwise in ½″-wide pieces
1 long red pepper, cut lengthwise and into ½″-wide pieces
2 long green peppers, cut lengthwise and into ½″-wide pieces
1 red potato, cut lengthwise and into ½″-wide pieces
¼ tsp of black pepper ground (optional)
Few sprigs of coriander for decoration

Method

1. Take a heavy-base pan and on medium heat. Add olive oil as soon as it is a little hot and add cumin seeds and mustard seeds. As soon as these start fluttering a little, add the onion. When it begins to turn pink, add garlic, ginger and lemon pieces and stir these for 3 to 4 minutes with a wooden stepula. Then, add turmeric, salt and chilli and stir for a minute or so.
2. At this point, all vegetables should be added to the pan. These should be nicely combined with all the stuff that is in the pan so that the vegetables are coated completely. After 5 minutes, gently turn them over being careful not to break them. If heat seems high, it can be reduced to low. Potatoes should be checked if these are soft to touch. As soon as these are soft, the dish will be ready.
3. Transfer this to a big round platter and black pepper should be sprinkled on top.
4. For garnishing, evenly spread some coriander leaves over the dish.

VEGETABLES

STEAMED CABBAGE AND BROAD BEAN

Preparation time: 15 minutes   Cooking time: 10 minutes   Total time: 25 minutes   Serves: 4

Ingredients

450 g of Cornish sweetheart cabbage, washed and cut into 1″-wide long strips
200 g of frozen and defrosted broad beans
2″ butter melted or 2 tbsp of ghee
¾ tsp of rock salt
½ tsp of finely ground pepper
¼ tsp of flaked red pepper (optional)
Few round strips of red pepper or a few cherry tomatoes, cut in half

Method

1. Add water to the lower part of the steamer and keep it on high heat. As soon as the water starts boiling, add cabbage and broad beans in separate pans and place them on the top of the boiling pot. Then reduce the heat to medium.
2. Let these boil. Broad beans should be ready in 5 to 6 minutes. When the beans are soft, take them out of the pan, place them in a bowl and set them aside. After another 2 to 3 minutes, switch off the heat of the pan that has cabbage. Mix the cabbage with the beans.
3. Add salt and pepper and mix them again. Finally, add butter or ghee and mix again.
4. Decorate this with pepper or cherry tomatoes.

VEGETABLES

ROASTED SQUASH WITH TURMERIC CHICKPEAS

| Preparation time: 15 minutes | Cooking time: 40 minutes | Total time: 55 minutes | Serves: 4 |

Ingredients

- **2 pounds of butternut squash,** seeds removed, cut into 1½" pieces
- **6 tbsp of cold-pressed coconut oil or any oil** of your choice
- **10 sprigs of fresh thyme**
- **1 tsp of rock salt,** more can be added to taste
- **½ tsp of black pepper,** finely ground

Turmeric chickpeas

- **1 medium-sized onion,** thinly sliced
- **1½ pieces ginger,** peeled and grated
- **4 cloves of garlic,** cut into small pieces
- **3 tbsp of apple cider vinegar**
- **1 can of chickpeas,** drained **(240 g)** can add more if preferred
- **2 tsp of ground turmeric**
- **1 cup of mixed fresh herbs, such as dill, parsley and mint,** coarsely cut
- **3 cups of rocket leaves salad**
- **½ cup of whole milk yogurt**
- **¼ cup of pomegranate seeds**

Method

1. Preheat the oven to 220°C.
2. Take a big oven tray and cover it with a large baking sheet. Add the squash pieces with 2 tbsps of oil, salt and pepper. Roast the squash until the pieces are tender and just beginning to turn golden brown. It may take 35 to 40 minutes.
3. Toss the onion, garlic, ginger, turmeric and vinegar in a large bowl and let them marinate for 10 to 12 minutes. Add the chickpeas and the remaining oil, and stir them nicely. Toss in half the herbs and season with salt and pepper.
4. Spread the rocket leaves on a large platter and add the roasted squash pieces. Then spread the marinated chickpeas and yogurt on top. Garnish with the remaining salad leaves and pomegranate seeds.

Special Note

1. Squash can be roasted, and chickpeas can also be marinated a couple of days in advance.

VEGETABLES
STIR-FRY CRISPY TOFU AND BLISTERED SNAP PEAS WITH CASHEWS

Preparation time: 10 minutes   Cooking time: 20 minutes   Total time: 30 minutes   Serves: 4

Ingredients

400 g of firm tofu, drained
3 tbsp of extra virgin olive oil or any neutral oil
⅓ tsp of fine rock salt, more can be added to taste
½ tsp ground pepper
½ cup of toasted cashews

Snap peas

1 pound of snap peas, trimmed
1" ginger, grated
2 cloves of garlic, cut into thin pieces
400 ml of coconut milk
1 tbsp of soy sauce
2 tsp of dark brown sugar or honey
1 tbsp of rice vinegar
4 spring onions, sliced and thinly sliced
¼ to ½ tsp of red chilli flakes (optional)
¼ cup of mint leaves, coarsely cut

Method

1. Slice the tofu in half horizontally. Leave it on a paper towel for a couple of minutes so that any excess liquid can be dried.
2. Season both sides of the tofu with salt and pepper.
3. In a heavy-based pan, add 1 tbsp oil and keep it over a medium heat until it starts simmering. Add tofu pieces to the pan. These should be kept in the pan until they are browned on both sides. This process can take approximately 8 minutes in total. When ready, they should be moved to a plate and set aside.
4. Using the same pan, add 1 tbsp of oil and keep it over medium heat. As soon as it starts shimmering, snap peas should be added. These should be stirred continuously until blistered and just tender, about 3 to 4 minutes. Season with salt and pepper and move to a bowl.
5. The same pan can be used. Add the remaining oil to the pan, then add ginger and garlic, and cook for 30 seconds. Pour in the coconut milk, soy sauce and sugar or honey if used. This should be stirred frequently until the sauce reduces. It may take 6 to 8 minutes. The sauce should be thick enough to coat a spoon without running off.
6. Tofu should be cut into 1" pieces. Tofu pieces and cashews should be added to the pan and stirred so that they are coated with the sauce. Remove from heat and taste to see if more salt is required.
7. Toss the snap peas with vinegar, spring onion, mint and red chilli flakes, if used.
8. Take a big platter. Add tofu pieces in half of the platter and snap peas in the other half.
9. Serve while it is hot.

Special Note

1. Serve with brown or white rice.

VEGETABLES

VEGETABLES

PANEER SUBZ BAHAR

| Preparation time: 15 minutes | Cooking time: 20 minutes | Total time: 35 minutes | Serves: 4 to 6 |

Ingredients

300 g of paneer, cut into tiny pieces
1 large onion, 4 cloves of garlic and 1½″ ginger, chopped in a food processor or cut into tiny pieces
1 red chilli, chopped or cut into small pieces (optional)
1 red pepper, cut into small pieces
1 carrot, cut into small pieces
½ cup of frozen peas
Few pieces of broccoli, cut into small pieces

Masala or tadka

2 tbsp of ghee or any oil of your choice
½″ of unwaxed lemon rind, nicely grated
2 tsp of tomato puree
½ a can of chopped tomatoes, approximately 250 g or **3 medium-sized tomatoes,** chopped in a food processor
1 tbsp of dry fenugreek leaves (methi)
¾ tsp of turmeric powder
1 tsp of cumin seeds
½ tsp of black mustard seeds
1 tsp of coriander powder
1 tsp of rock salt, more can be added after tasting
1 tsp of garam masala (optional)
Few sprigs of fresh coriander, cut into small pieces, coarsely

Method

1. Take a large heavy-bottom pan and keep on medium heat, then add ghee or oil of your choice. When the ghee gets a little hot, add cumin and mustard seeds. As soon as these start bubbling, add the mixture of onion, ginger and garlic and cook these for 7 to 8 minutes stirring often. Once the colour changes to light brown, add turmeric, salt, coriander powder and fenugreek leaves. Then add chopped tomatoes, tomato puree, lemon rind and chilli and mix these nicely. At this point, reduce the heat to low and cover the pan so that the tomatoes combine properly and turn into a smooth paste. This takes 8 to 10 minutes. This paste should be stirred occasionally so that it does not get burned.
2. Add pepper, carrot and broccoli and mix these properly. Let it simmer for 10 to 12 minutes until the vegetables become a little tender. Add peas, mix again and cover the pan, and leave it for another 5 minutes.
3. Add the paneer pieces and let them simmer for 10 minutes, stirring continuously.
4. Finally, switch off the heat and sprinkle garam masala, and cover it so that the flavour is retained.
5. Sprinkle fresh coriander before serving.

Special Notes

1. Serve with plain rice, jeera rice or chapatis.
2. Oil can be used to make the recipe **vegan**.

VEGETABLES

VEGETABLES

BAKED SPINACH AND CHEESE

Preparation time: 5 minutes   Cooking time: 10 minutes   Total time: 15 minutes   Serves: 4

Ingredients

300 g of baby spinach, washed and dried in a salad spinner
3 cloves of garlic, pressed
¾ tsp of rock salt, more can be added to taste
¼ tsp of black pepper, finely ground
3 tbsp of extra virgin olive oil
80 g of grated mozzarella cheese or any other cheese can be used

Method

1. Preheat the oven to 250°C. I use an electric oven that has the fan option.
2. Take a shallow oven dish. Add spinach, garlic, salt, pepper and oil. Mix it completely and put it in the oven for 5 minutes.
3. Take it out, mix it again and keep it back for another 5 minutes.
4. Take it out, mix it again and sprinkle cheese on the top.
5. Change the setting to grill and when it is heated, keep the tray under the grill for 5 minutes or until the colour of the cheese changes to light brown.
6. Take out the dish and enjoy. This dish is enjoyed most when it is piping hot.

Menu suggestion: This can be served with fish, thin-cut baked potatoes and salad.

VEGETABLES

BAKED SWEDE AND LEEK

| Preparation time: 15 minutes | Cooking time: 35 minutes | Total time: 50 minutes | Serves: 4 |

Ingredients

1 large swede, cut into 2 cm chunks
1 large leek, thinly cut
4 tbsp of extra virgin olive oil
1 tsp of rye/mustard seeds
1 tsp of rock salt, more can be added to taste
¼ tsp of haldi/turmeric powder
1 large red chilli, cut into small round pieces (optional)
¼ tsp of red chilli flakes (optional)
¼ tsp of black pepper, finely ground

Method

1. Preheat the oven at 220°C. I use the electric oven which has the fan option.
2. Take a shallow oven dish. Add swede, salt, pepper, chilli, red chilli and 3 tbsp of the oil. Mix it nicely and put it in the oven for 30 minutes or until nearly done tossing occasionally.
3. Keep a heavy-based pan on medium heat, add remaining oil and as soon as it becomes a little hot, add rye seeds.
4. As soon as it starts bubbling, add haldi, pinch of salt, stir it a little and add leeks.
5. Stir-fry for 2 to 3 minutes until it gets a little soft.
6. Add the swede pieces and mix these completely.
7. Sprinkle black pepper and serve.
8. This is enjoyed most when it is piping hot.

VEGETABLES

BHINDI SABJI (OKRA STIR FRIED)

| Preparation time: 10 minutes | Cooking time: 20 minutes | Total time: 30 minutes | Serves: 4 to 6 |

Bhindi ki sabji is one of the tastiest Indian-style recipes, and it is ready in 30 minutes.

INGREDIENTS

2 tbsp of olive oil or any other oil of your choice
1 tsp of jeera (cumin seeds)
½ tsp of black rye (mustard seeds)
½ tsp of haldi (turmeric powder)
1 large onion, sliced
500 g of bhindi, cut into small pieces
1 green or red chilli, cut into small pieces (optional)
¼ tsp of red chilli flakes (optional)
1 tbsp rind of unwaxed lemon, grated or cut into small pieces
1 tsp of lemon juice
½ tsp garam masala
½ tsp of rock salt, more can be added as per your choice

METHOD

1. Wash and dry the Bhindi in advance so that no moisture is left. To avoid any moisture, they should be dried with kitchen paper or a kitchen cloth. Once completely dry, then cut them into small pieces.
2. Keep the pan on medium heat. As soon as it becomes hot, add jeera and rye seeds. As soon as they start bubbling, add onion and continue stirring until they are light pink.
3. Add turmeric, and after a few seconds, add bhindi, lemon rind and lemon juice, and combine them nicely. The pan can be covered for a couple of minutes. Then leave it uncovered for the next 12 to 15 minutes until the bhindi pieces become soft. Add green and red chilli and combine them properly. These should be stirred occasionally so that they do not stick to the pan.
3. Add salt just when the bhindi is ready.
5. Take it out in a bowl, sprinkle garam masala and cover it.

SPECIAL NOTES

1. Make sure that the bhindi is dry before you cut it.
2. Don't add any water during the cooking process.
3. Add salt towards the end when the okra is cooked.
4. Serve with chapatis or prantha and enjoy.

VEGETABLES

STIR-FRY GAJAR (CARROT), ALOO (POTATO) AND METHI (FENUGREEK LEAVES)

| Preparation time: 35 minutes | Cooking time: 20 minutes | Total time: 55 minutes | Serves: 4 to 6 |

Ingredients

3 tbsp of extra virgin olive oil
1 tsp of cumin seeds
½ tsp of mustard seeds
1 onion, 1½″ ginger and 2 cloves of garlic, cut into small pieces
1 small green chilli cut into small pieces (optional)
½ tsp of turmeric
1 tsp of rock salt, more can be added as per the taste
4 carrots, cut into small rounds
2 big red potatoes, cut into ½″ pieces
1 bunch of fresh methi, chopped finely (fenugreek leaves)
½ cup of peas, shelled (frozen can also be used)
½ tsp of garam masala

Method

1. Take a heavy-based pan and keep on medium heat. Add olive oil. As soon as it is a little hot, add cumin seeds and mustard seeds. As soon as these start fluttering a little, add onion. When the onion starts turning into pink, add garlic and ginger and stir these for 2 to 3 minutes with a wooden spatula. Add turmeric and salt and stir for another minute.
2. At this point, add methi leaves and mix them nicely and go on stirring it for 5 to 7 minutes. Then add carrots, potatoes, peas and chilli and mix them completely. Reduce the heat to low and cover the pan, stirring occasionally so that it does not stick to the bottom. After 8 to 10 minutes, check the potato and carrot, and if these have become soft, the vegetable is ready.
3. It should be transferred to a medium-sized bowl, and garam masala should be sprinkled. The bowl should be covered to keep the aroma.

Special Note

1. Gajar methi vegetable is best enjoyed with chapatis and yogurt raita.

VEGETABLES

BAKED FLAT BEANS

Preparation time: 15 minutes | Cooking time: 10 minutes | Total time: 25 minutes | Serves: 4

Ingredients

300 g of flat beans, trimmed at both ends
½ **tsp of rock salt**
3 **tbsp of olive oil**
3 **tbsp of lemon juice**
2 **tbsp of fresh mint leaves**
½ **tsp of pepper,** coarsely ground

Method

1. Add water to the lower part of the steamer and keep it on high heat. As soon as it starts boiling, reduce the heat to medium and add flat beans. Season with a little salt and steam for 6 minutes or until tender.
2. In the meantime, switch on the grill to a high setting. Grill them for 10 minutes, turning them once. Some of these should have turned a little brown.
3. Remove the beans from the grill and place them on a serving plate.
4. In a small bowl, add olive oil, lemon juice, salt and pepper. Lemon juice will give the dressing a tangy flavour. If required, add more salt as per your liking. Add the dressing to the flat beans so that they are nicely covered.
5. Scatter fresh mint leaves over the dish and serve immediately.

VEGETABLES

STIR-FRY PARSNIP AND LEEK

| Preparation time: 10 minutes | Cooking time: 15 minutes | Total time: 25 minutes | Serves: 4 to 6 |

Ingredients

500 g of parsnip, peeled and cut into small rounds
3 tbsp of olive oil
1 tsp of cumin seeds
½ tsp of black mustard seeds
1½″ ginger, grated
4 cloves of garlic, cut into tiny pieces
½ tsp of turmeric powder
½ tsp of rock salt
1 green chilli, cut into small rounds (optional)
¼ tsp of red chilli flakes (optional)
300 g of leeks, cut into thin strips
¼ tsp of garam masala

Method

1. Add water to the lower part of the steamer and keep it on high heat. As soon as it starts boiling, reduce the heat to medium and add parsnips. Steam these for 6 minutes or until tender. Take them out from the steamer and set aside.
2. In the meantime, make the tadka. Take a heavy-based frying pan and keep it on medium heat. Add oil, and as soon as it gets a little hot, add cumin and mustard seeds. When it starts bubbling, add garlic and ginger and mix them nicely. When they turn into light pink, add turmeric and salt and stir well. Add leeks and mix well, then cover the pan. Reduce the heat and leave it for 3 to 5 minutes.
3. Add parsnip pieces to the pan and mix them completely. Add green chilli and chilli flakes and mix again. The heat should be reduced to low. Leave it on the fire for another 2 to 3 minutes.
4. Sprinkle garam masala and cover it to retain the aroma.
5. Serve hot.

VEGETABLES

ALOO PALAK (POTATO SPINACH)

| Preparation time: 10 minutes | Cooking time: 20 minutes | Total time: 30 minutes | Serves: 4 to 6 |

Ingredients

500 g of spinach leaves, cut coarsely
2 large russet potatoes, peeled and cut into 2 cm cubes
2 tbsp of ghee or butter
1 onion, finely chopped
1 tbsp of ginger, chopped
2 cloves of garlic, sliced
1 medium-sized tomato, cut into small pieces
1 to 2 green chillies, cut into small rounds (optional)
1 tsp of cumin seeds
½ tsp of black mustard seeds
½ tsp of turmeric
1 tsp of rock salt, more can be added to taste
½ tsp of garam masala

Method

1. Take a heavy-base pan and keep it on medium heat. Add ghee once it is slightly hot. Then add cumin and mustard seeds. As soon as these start fluttering, add the onion. When they start turning pink, add garlic and ginger and stir these for 2 to 3 minutes with a wooden spatula. Add turmeric and salt and stir for a minute or so.
2. Add the tomato, stir it with the onion mixture and leave it for 2 to 3 minutes more.
3. Add potatoes and chillies, mix them nicely, and cover the pan for 5 minutes, reducing the heat. Stir a couple of times to avoid sticking to the base.
4. Add spinach, mix it completely with the mixture and cover it for 2 to 3 minutes. Once the spinach leaves become soft and the potatoes are nearly cooked, uncover the pan, increase the heat to a higher setting and leave it on until the water has evaporated.
5. It is ready to be served as soon as the water has evaporated. It should be transferred to a medium-sized bowl and sprinkled with garam masala. Keep the bowl covered to preserve the aroma.

Special Notes

1. Aloo palak is best enjoyed with chapatis and yogurt raita.
2. Coconut oil can be used to make it **vegan**.

VEGETABLES

MIXED VEGETABLE BAKE

| Preparation time: 15 minutes | Cooking time: 25 minutes | Total time: 40 minutes | Serves: 4 to 5 |

Ingredients

1 big sweet potato, cut into ½″ cubes
4 small round potatoes, cut into thin round pieces
2 medium-sized courgettes, cut into thin round pieces
2 red peppers, cut into 2″ strips
1 big onion, cut into thin slices
4 cloves of garlic, cut into very thin slices
1¼ tsp of sea salt
½ tsp of black pepper, finely ground
½ tsp of turmeric powder
½ tsp of red chilli flakes (optional)
1½ tsp of dried rosemary
3 to 4 tbsp of olive oil

Method

1. Preheat the oven to 220 °C. I use an electric oven that has the fan option.
2. Take a shallow oven dish. Add all the above ingredients, mix these nicely and put them in the preheated oven for 20 minutes.
3. After 20 minutes, these should be mixed nicely and kept in the oven for another 5 minutes or until they are nicely done.
4. At this point, it is ready to be eaten as a side.
5. It is enjoyed when it is piping hot.

VEGETABLES

ALOO (POTATO) BAINGAN (AUBERGINE) SABJI

Preparation time: 10 minutes   Cooking time: 25 minutes   Total time: 35 minutes   Serves: 4

Ingredients

300 g of potatoes, peeled and sliced lengthwise to ½″ thickness. Keep them immersed in a bowl of water until used
350 g of baingan, sliced to 1″ thickness

Masala or tadka

⅔ **tbsp of ghee or any oil** of your choice
1 tsp of cumin seeds
½ tsp of black mustard seeds
1 large onion, 3 cloves of garlic and 1½″ ginger, chopped in a food processor or cut into tiny pieces
¾ tsp of turmeric powder
1 tsp of rock salt, more can be added after tasting
½ a can of chopped tomatoes, approximately 250 g or 3 medium-sized tomatoes, chopped in a food processor or cut into small pieces
2 tsp of tomato puree
½″ of unwaxed lemon rind, nicely grated
1 red chilli, chopped or cut into small pieces (optional)
1 tsp of garam masala
Few sprigs of fresh coriander, cut into small pieces, coarsely
Little water if required

Method

1. Take a large heavy-bottom frying pan and keep it on medium heat. Add ghee. When the ghee gets a little hot, add cumin and mustard seeds. As soon as it starts bubbling, add the mixture of onion, ginger and garlic and cook these for 3 to 5 minutes stirring often. Add turmeric and salt.
2. Add tomato, tomato puree, lemon rind and chilli and mix these nicely. At this point, reduce the heat to low and cover the pan so that the tomatoes combine properly and turn into a smooth paste. This takes 5 to 7 minutes. This paste should be stirred occasionally so that it does not get stuck to the pan.
3. Remove the sliced potatoes from the water and add them to the pan. Stir-fry for 2 to 3 minutes until they look slightly transparent.
4. Lower the heat and cook them, covered, until half cooked. They will be slightly tender but still undercooked at this stage.
5. Then add the baingan pieces to the pan. Stir-fry for 2 to 3 minutes until the skin of these discolours.
6. If required, a couple of tbsp of water can be added to avoid the vegetables sticking to the pan.
7. Cover the pan and cook on low heat until the potatoes are completely cooked and fork-tender but not mushy. While cooking, stir occasionally to prevent them from burning.
8. Sprinkle garam masala and cover the pan so that the aroma is retained.
9. Sprinkle fresh coriander before serving.

Special Notes

1. Serve with plain rice, jeera rice or chapatis.
2. Oil can be used to make the recipe **vegan**.

VEGETABLES

VEGETABLES

SAG

Preparation time: 45 minutes Cooking time: 35 minutes Total time: 80 minutes Serves: 4 to 6

Ingredients

200 g of curly kale
300 g of spinach leaves
300 g of sliced greens
½ leek, cut into small pieces
1" ginger, cut into thin, big pieces
2 whole cloves of garlic
1 whole green chilli (optional)
1 tsp of sea salt, more can be added after tasting
¾ tsp of turmeric powder
1 tbsp of ghee
½ cup of water
2 tbsp of besan

Masala or tadka
2 tbsp of ghee or any oil as per your choice
1 tsp of cumin seeds
½ tsp of black mustard seeds
1 large onion, 4 cloves of garlic and 1½" ginger, cut into tiny pieces
1 tsp of tomato puree
½ can of chopped tomatoes, approximately 250 g or 2 medium-sized tomatoes cut into small pieces
1 green chilli, chopped or cut into small pieces (optional)
½ tsp of red chilli flakes (optional)
½ tsp of garam masala

Method

To pressure-cook

1. Wash all 4 vegetables in running water at least 3 times and add them to a medium-sized pressure cooker.
2. Add ginger, cloves, chilli, salt, turmeric powder, ghee and water except besan and give 2 whistles.
3. Let it cool on its own.
4. When it cools down, add besan and put in a blender. Blend it until it is smooth.
5. Set aside.

Masala or tadka

1. Take a medium heavy-based pan and keep it on medium heat.
2. Add ghee. When the ghee gets a little hot, add cumin and mustard seeds. As soon as it starts bubbling, add the mixture of onion, ginger and garlic and cook these for 5 to 6 minutes, stirring often. Once the colour changes to light pink, add chopped tomato and tomato puree, green chilli and red chilli flakes. Mix these nicely. At this point, reduce the heat to low and cover the pan so that the tomatoes combine properly and it turns into a smooth paste. This paste should be stirred occasionally so that it does not get burned.
3. The consistency of the paste should be like yogurt.
4. Add blended vegetables to the masala and combine them thoroughly. The heat should be kept on low and the pan should be covered. It should be left on the fire for another 10 to 15 minutes, stirring occasionally until the excess water evaporates.
5. Add garam masala and cover it for a couple of minutes so that the flavour is retained.

Special Notes

1. Serve with plain rice, jeera rice or chapatis and enjoy.
2. Oil can be used to make the recipe **vegan**.

VEGETABLES

VEGETABLES

BAINGAN KA BHARTA (AUBERGINE MASH)

Preparation time: 15 minutes   Cooking time: 30 minutes   Total time: 45 minutes   Serves: 4

Ingredients

For roasting
2 medium-sized baingan
Little oil to rub on these – sunflower oil

Other Ingredients
2 tbsp of oil – any oil can be used
1 tsp of jeera
½ tsp of black rai
1 tej patta
2 medium-sized onions, cut into small pieces
2 tsp of grated ginger
4 cloves of garlic, cut into small pieces
2 medium-sized tomatoes, finely chopped
1 tsp of tomato puree
1 green chilli (optional)
¼ tsp of red flake chilli (optional)
1 tsp of ground coriander
1 tsp of sea salt, more can be added as per taste
1 tbsp of kasuri dry methi
½ tsp garam masala
Few sprigs of fresh coriander leaves, cut coarsely

Method

1. For roasting, wash the baingan and dry them with paper. Then rub oil on both the baingan and keep them directly on the gas fire. Keep turning it after every 2 to 3 minutes. You will see that the skin starts splitting and the inner side of the baingan becomes visible. It will feel softer when touched. It may take 10 to 12 minutes to completely roast them. Once they are fully roasted, put them in a big bowl of cold water for 5 minutes.
2. After 5 minutes, take these out of the water, peel them and mash them completely. Then set aside.
3. Take a heavy-based pan and keep on medium heat. Add oil, and as soon as it starts bubbling, add jeera, rai and tej patta.
4. Soon after, add onion, ginger and garlic. Cook these for 5 to 6 minutes, stirring often. Once the colour changes to light pink, add chopped tomato, tomato puree, green chilli, red chilli, coriander and salt and mix these nicely. At this point, reduce the heat to low and cover the pan so that the tomatoes are combined properly and it turns into a smooth paste. This paste should be stirred occasionally so that it does not get burned.
5. Then add mashed baingan and sprinkle kasuri methi as well. Stir these nicely and leave it uncovered, continuing to stir every 2 to 3 minutes.
6. It should look roasted and there should be no water visible in the pan. After 10 minutes, half of the coriander should be added and stirred for a few more minutes.
7. Delicious bharta should be ready. A little garam masala and remaining coriander should be sprinkled on it for decoration.
8. Finally, bharta can be enjoyed with hot chapatis or rice.

VEGETABLES

VEGETABLES

BAKED BUTTERNUT SQUASH

| Preparation time: 25 minutes | Cooking time: 30 minutes | Total time: 55 minutes | Serves: 4 to 5 |

Ingredients

1 butternut squash approximately 650 g cut into 1″ pieces
4 cloves of garlic, cut into thin slices
1¼ tsp of sea salt
½ tsp of black pepper, finely ground
½ tsp of turmeric powder
½ tsp of red chilli flakes (optional)
1½ tsp of dried rosemary
3 to 4 tbsp of olive oil

Method

1. Preheat the oven to 220°C. I use an electric oven, which has a fan option.
2. Take a shallow oven dish. Add butternut squash, garlic, salt, pepper, turmeric powder, chilli, rosemary and 3 tbsp of the oil. Mix it nicely and put it in the preheated oven for 30 minutes or until nearly done, tossing occasionally.
3. Once these are soft to the touch, they can be moved to the grill for 8 to 10 minutes so that they get some brownish marks.
4. This is ready to eat as a side with a main meal.
5. It is enjoyed most when it is piping hot.

SALADS

SALADS

WALNUT AND TOMATO SALAD WITH POMEGRANATE MOLASSES

Preparation time: 15 minutes   Cooking time: 5 minutes   Total time: 20 minutes

Ingredients

150 g of crushed walnuts
1 onion, cut into small pieces
1 beef tomato, cut into small pieces
Few sprigs of parsley, cut coarsely into small pieces

Dressing

1 tbsp of pomegranate molasses
¼ cup of olive oil
½ tsp of rock salt, more can be added as per taste
¼ tsp of finely ground black pepper

Method

1. Take a heavy-based frying pan and keep it on medium heat. Add the walnuts and make sure that they are in a single layer. Stir them continuously for 2 to 3 minutes until the nuts become fragrant. Set the nuts aside to cool.
2. Take a medium-sized bowl, add onion, tomato and parsley and then add the nuts and gently fold these.
3. In a separate bowl, whisk the pomegranate molasses, olive oil, salt and pepper.
4. Drizzle the dressing over the walnut mixture and combine these nicely.
5. You can finish with a few grinds of fresh pepper.

SALADS
ROCKET SALAD WITH AVOCADO AND CHERRY TOMATOES

Preparation time: 20 minutes   Total time: 20 minutes   Serves: 4

Ingredients

100 g of rocket salad
2 medium avocados, cut into halves, then cut into thin slices
125 g of cherry tomatoes, washed
2 tbsp of flaxseed oil
½ tsp of rock salt
¼ tsp of pepper
1 tbsp of milled organic flaxseed

Method

1. Take a medium-sized bowl.
2. Add rocket leaves, salt, pepper and flaxseed and mix these properly.
3. Then add the oil and mix it again.
4. Once properly mixed, spread it on a large plate, then spread avocado pieces on top of the leaves. In the end, add cherry tomatoes on the top.

SALADS

MANGO, AVOCADO, POMEGRANATE AND WALNUT PIECES

Preparation time: 15 minutes   Total time: 15 minutes   Serves: 4

Ingredients

2 mangoes, cut into slices
2 avocados, cut into slices
40 g of pomegranate seeds
15 pieces of half walnuts
½ tsp of flaked rock salt
¼ tsp of pepper, finely ground
3 tbsp of extra virgin olive oil
1 tbsp of apple cider, raw organic

Method

1. Take a large round plate and spread mango and avocado slices evenly.
2. On the top, add walnut pieces, pomegranate seeds and sprinkle salt, pepper, olive oil and vinegar.
3. The dish is ready to serve.

SALADS

BABY CUCUMBERS AND LETTUCE

Preparation time: 20 minutes   Total time: 20 minutes   Serves: 4

Ingredients

6 baby cucumbers
50 g of lamb's lettuce
10 g of mint leaves
10 g of coriander leaves
1 tsp of nigella seeds

Dressing

1 tbsp of lemon juice
1 clove of garlic, crushed
3 cm piece of ginger, finely grated
25 g of plain yogurt, nicely mixed so that it becomes smooth
½ tsp of fine rock salt

Method

1. Mix all the ingredients for dressing and keep aside.
2. Cut the cucumbers into quarters lengthways. Then cut each long quarter diagonally into 2 or 3 cm slices and place them in a large bowl. Next, add the lamb lettuce, mint and coriander and mix these. Dressing can be added and mixed gently. Once mixed, this should be spread in a large shallow bowl. Sprinkle with the nigella seeds and serve.

SALADS

BEEF TOMATO WITH SPRING ONION AND GINGER SAUCE

Preparation time: 15 minutes | Cooking time: 5 minutes | Total time: 20 minutes | Serves: 4

Ingredients

3 big fully ripe beef tomatoes, sliced to 2 mm thickness
3″ ginger, peeled and chopped
¾ **tsp of rock salt**
4 spring onions, finely sliced
4 tbsp of extra virgin olive oil, a little more for finishing
2 tbsp of organic apple cider organic vinegar
¼ **green chilli,** deseeded and finely chopped
2 tbsp of finely shredded coriander

Method

1. Put the ginger and ½ tsp of salt into a pestle and mortar and crush to a fine paste. Transfer to a bowl and keep aside.
2. Take a small pan and keep it on low heat. Add 3 tsp of oil. As soon as it gets hot, add spring onion and 1 tsp of vinegar. Stir together and leave it for a minute. Switch it off and keep it aside.
3. Take a large platter and lay the tomato slices slightly overlapping. Season with the remaining salt and drizzle the remaining vinegar on top. Then, using your hands, spread the spring onion and ginger mix evenly over the tomatoes and scatter the chilli and finish with the remaining olive oil.

SALADS

EGG, AVOCADO, ROCKET LEAVES WITH POMEGRANATE AND FLAXSEED OIL

Preparation time: 20 minutes   Total time: 20 minutes   Serves: 4

Ingredients

4 eggs, hard-boiled, cut into halves
2 avocados, cut into halves
100 g of rocket leaves
50 g of pomegranate seeds
2 tbsp of flaxseed oil
½ tsp of flaked rock salt
¼ tsp of black pepper, finely ground

Method

1. Take a large round plate and spread rocket leaves evenly all over the plate.
2. Add egg and avocado pieces over the leaves.
3. Scatter pomegranate seeds evenly.
4. Sprinkle salt, pepper and oil nicely so that everything is covered.

SALADS

SUGAR SNAP PEAS WITH FETA, DILL AND YOGURT

| Preparation time: 20 minutes | Cooking time: 5 minutes | Total time: 25 minutes | Serves: 4 |

Ingredients

½ **pound of sugar snap peas,** trimmed
1 **clove of garlic,** finely grated
2 **tbsp of fresh lemon juice**
4 **tbsp of extra virgin olive oil,** plus a little bit more for drizzling
1 **cup of thinly sliced radish**
½ **cup of dill,** chopped coarsely
2 **spring onions,** thinly sliced
½ **cup of whole milk yogurt**
½ **cup of feta,** crumbled
½ **tsp of finely grated lemon zest**
For serving, **a few mint and parsley leaves**
¼ **tsp of fine rock salt,** plus more for adding to the water
¼ **tsp of black pepper,** finely ground

Method

1. Keep a large pot of water to boil with a little salt. At the same time, keep a bowl of salted ice water and a slotted spoon in hand. As soon as the water starts boiling, drop peas into the boiling water and cook until they are tender but still crisp. These should be ready within a minute. Use the slotted spoon to transfer the peas to ice water to cool completely. Drain well and pat dry with a kitchen towel.
2. When cool enough, put the peas on a cutting board and slice them in half, crosswise.
3. Take a bowl and add garlic and lemon juice, and whisk together. Stir in salt and pepper. Whisk in 3 tbsp of olive oil. Add the peas, spring onions, mint and parsley leaves, and toss well. After tasting, add more lemon juice, olive oil and salt if required.
4. In a small bowl, add yogurt, feta, lemon zest and the remaining olive oil. Add salt, pepper and lemon juice to taste.
5. Take a serving platter and spread the yogurt mixture on it. Then spoon the peas on half of the platter and feta on the other half and drizzle with oil and herbs.

Special Note

1. This can be served as a side dish or eaten as an appetizer with crispy bread.

SALADS

GRILLED BEEF TOMATO WITH CHILLI AND BASIL LEAVES

| Preparation time: 15 minutes | Cooking time: 15 minutes | Total time: 30 minutes | Serves: 4 |

Ingredients

4 big fully ripe beef tomatoes, cut into thin round slices
4 tbsp of extra virgin olive oil
3 mild red chillies, sliced into ½ cm rounds (if you want to make it milder, seeds should be taken out)
6 cloves of garlic, thinly sliced
4 cm piece of ginger, finely cut into thin strips
25 g of basil leaves, cut coarsely; 5 g leaves to be kept for garnish
1½ tsp of mustard seeds
1 tsp of flaked rock salt
½ tsp of finely ground black pepper

Method

1. Preheat the oven to 250 °C.
2. Take a heavy-based saucepan and keep it on medium heat. When it is a little warm, add oil, and as soon as it gets hot, add ginger, garlic and chillies and fry gently for 2 minutes, stirring occasionally until the garlic starts turning a little pink. Add mustard seeds, and as soon as they start bubbling, add basil leaves and continue to fry for another 1 to 2 minutes. Take a slotted spoon and transfer the mixture to a bowl to stop it from cooking and keep the remaining aromatic oil separately.
3. Arrange the tomato slices on a large baking tray, taking care that they do not overlap. Brush the slices with the prepared aromatic oil and then sprinkle them with salt and pepper. Place the tray under the grill taking care that it is not very near to the heat. It should be at least 4 to 5 cm away from the direct heat. Cook for 10 to 12 minutes until the tomatoes have started to brown. Remove the tray from the oven, sprinkle the remaining oil over the tomatoes and keep it aside for 10 minutes.
4. After 10 minutes, these should be transferred to a large platter, overlapping them slightly. Scatter the basil leaves and mustard seeds mixture and any leftover oil and juices over them. This should be served warm to enjoy it fully.

SALADS
AVOCADO, CHERRY TOMATOES AND ROCKET LEAVES

Preparation time: 15 minutes   Total time: 15 minutes   Serves: 4

Ingredients

2 avocados, cut into slices
300 g of cherry tomatoes
150 g of rocket leaves
½ **tsp of flaked rock salt**
¼ **tsp pepper,** finely ground
3 tbsp of extra virgin olive oil
1 tbsp of milled flaxseed and walnut

Method

1. Take a large round plate, spread rocket leaves so that the plate is fully covered.
2. Spread avocado slices and cherry tomatoes evenly.
3. Sprinkle salt, pepper and milled flaxseed and walnut mixture and top it with olive oil.
4. The dish is ready to serve.

SALADS
SWEET POTATOES, CHICKPEAS, SPINACH AND POMEGRANATE

Preparation time: 15 minutes | Cooking time: 15 minutes | Total time: 30 minutes | Serves: 4

Ingredients

2 big sweet potatoes, boiled, peeled and cut into small cubes
200 g of boiled chickpeas (half of 400 g can)
200 g of spinach leaves, cut into strips
50 g of pomegranate seeds
3 tbsp of extra virgin olive oil
¼ tsp of rock salt
¼ tsp of pepper
1 tbsp of milled flaxseed and walnut

Method

1. Take a medium-sized bowl. Add sweet potatoes and chickpeas, then season with salt, pepper and oil. Mix everything well and set aside.
2. Take a small bowl and add spinach strips, coating them with oil. Add the spinach to the sweet potato mixture.
3. Sprinkle with milled flaxseed and walnut and pomegranate seeds, then serve.

SALADS

COURGETTE AND HERB SALAD WITH MOZZARELLA AND DUKKAH

| Preparation time: 20 minutes | Cooking time: 35 minutes | Total time: 55 minutes | Serves: 4 to 6 |

Dukkah ingredients

75 g of flaked almonds
75 g of sesame seeds
75 g of pumpkin seeds
75 g of sunflower seeds
2 tbsp of extra virgin olive oil
⅓ tbsp of flaky sea salt
2 tbsp of coriander seeds
2 tbsp of fennel seeds
1 tbsp of cumin seeds
½ tsp of chilli flakes

Method

1. Set the oven to preheat at 180 °C (fan oven).
2. Take a medium-sized baking tray and place the flaked almonds, sesame, pumpkin and sunflower seeds. Add the olive oil and salt and mix well so that all the seeds are well coated. Bake in the oven for 10 minutes.
3. Add the coriander, fennel and cumin seeds and mix again.
4. Return to the oven for another 10 minutes. After 10 minutes, remove from the oven and add chilli flakes. Leave it to cool. Once cooled, it can be stored in an airtight container.

Salad ingredients

5 tbsp of extra virgin olive oil
2 small courgettes, halved lengthways
A few sprigs of fresh basil
1 tbsp of butter
1 lemon, 1 slice cut into small pieces, and juice taken out of the rest
3 round pieces of mozzarella
3 to 4 tbsp of dukkah

Method

1. Keep a large, heavy-based frying pan on medium heat and add olive oil. Once it gets a little hot, add the courgettes and change the heat setting to high. Courgettes should be placed cut-side down and cooked for 3 to 4 minutes until they turn a golden colour.
2. Once one side is done, flip all the pieces so that the rounded side is facing down.
3. Add the slices of lemon and cook for a further 3 to 4 minutes. Then add the butter.
4. As soon as it is melted and starts sizzling, remove from heat and transfer to a large platter, then add the remaining juice and basil leaves, and top with mozzarella and the dukkah. It is ready to serve now.

Special Note

1. Dukkah can also be used as a delicious and nutritious snack.

SALADS

SALADS

SPROUTED MOONG DAL

Preparation time: 5 minutes   Cooking time: 15 minutes   Total time: 20 minutes   Serves: 4 to 6

Ingredients for preparation of sprouts

200 g of sabut moong dal
Enough water to soak it.
The sprouts can also be made in advance

Preparation for salad

200 g of sprouted dal
2 tbsp of olive oil
½ tsp of rye (mustard) seeds
1 onion, cut into tiny pieces
Few lemon wedges, with half to be kept for decoration
1 red chilli, cut into tiny round pieces (optional)
¼ tsp of red chilli flakes (optional)
¼ tsp of haldi (turmeric powder)
½ tsp of rock salt, more can be added as per taste
¼ tsp of pepper
1 tbsp of lemon juice
Few tbsp of water, if required
Few sprigs of coriander leaves cut coarsely, half to be added while preparing and half to be kept for decoration

Sprouts Preparation Method

1. Add dal to a medium-sized bowl. Rinse it 3 times and fill it up with water. Keep it overnight.
2. In the morning, take these out of the water and spread the sprouts evenly in both the containers of the sprout maker.
3. Close the top tightly and leave it for 24 to 36 hours until the dal starts sprouting.
4. Once sprouted, rinse it 2 to 3 times and keep it aside in a strainer so that most of the water comes out.
5. Sprouts can be made in advance and kept in the freezer and used as and when required.

Preparation for salad

6. Keep a heavy-based frying pan on medium heat. When it gets hot, add olive oil and soon after, add rye seeds.
7. As soon as these start bubbling, add onion, and as soon as the onion gets a little pink, add lemon wedges, haldi, salt, and soon after add sprouted moong and chilli. Stir these nicely. Cover the pan.
8. Reduce the heat and leave it covered for 5 to 7 minutes. If it starts sticking to the pan, 1 to 2 tbsp of water can be added.
9. After 10 minutes, check if these have become soft. If still hard, keep them on the heat for a few more minutes. Please make sure there is no water left.
10. Once soft, move it to a shallow plate and mix in half of the coriander, lemon juice and pepper.
11. Decorate it with the remaining coriander, lemon wedges and chilli pieces.

Special Note

1. Spices can be added in lesser or more as per your requirements.

SALADS

SALADS
AVOCADO AND CUCUMBER SALAD WITH FRIED HALLOUMI

| Preparation time: 20 minutes | Cooking time: 5 minutes | Total time: 25 minutes | Serves: 4 |

Ingredients

250 g of halloumi pack
6 tbsp of extra virgin olive oil
2 cloves of garlic, cut into small pieces
Few sprigs of parsley, cut coarsely
Few sprigs of mint
1 large cucumber
150 g of radishes
1 large avocado
Juice of two lemons
1 green chilli, deseeded and thinly sliced (optional)
4 spring onions, thinly sliced
¼ tsp of flaky rock salt
¼ tsp of black pepper, ground

Method

1. Dice the halloumi into 2 cm cubes and place them on kitchen paper.
2. Take a heavy-based pan and keep it on medium heat. Add 2 tbsp of oil to the pan, and once it gets hot, add the halloumi pieces. Keep turning them until they become golden brown. Remove from heat. Add garlic and toss these with halloumi pieces so that they are coated well. Sprinkle with pepper and add half of the chopped parsley and mint.
3. Cut the cucumber into 2 cm pieces, cut the radishes into small pieces and place them in a large bowl. Dice the avocado and add it to the cucumber and radish pieces. Add lemon juice and salt. Add chilli, spring onions and remaining herbs, and mix well.
4. Pour over the remaining olive oil and transfer to a large serving plate, topping with fried halloumi cheese. This dish should be served while the cheese is still warm.

Special Note

1. This dish can be served as a salad or light lunch.

SALADS

CARROT, MOOLI AND SPRING ONION WITH CAPERS

| Preparation time: 15 minutes | Cooking time: 5 minutes | Total time: 20 minutes | Serves: 4 |

At times, you fancy having a salad but not a cold one. For these times, there is a recipe for a warm one.

Ingredients

2 carrots, grated
10 red radishes, grated
½ unwaxed lemon, grated
Few strips of raw mango peel, grated (optional)
½ can (400 g) of chickpeas or kidney beans or frozen soya beans. Any type of beans can be used
1 bunch of spring onions, cut into small rounds
Few sprigs of parsley, cut coarsely
3 tbsp of extra virgin olive oil
¼ tsp of rock salt
¼ tsp of pepper
3 tbsp of capers, olives or gherkins, cut into small pieces. Any of these can be used

Method

1. Take a pan and keep it on medium heat. As soon as it gets hot, add carrot, radish, lemon and mango peel. Stir it and keep it on the heat for 2 to 3 minutes. Take it out in a salad bowl. Add beans to the same pan and keep on heat for 2 minutes. After 2 minutes, mix it with the carrot mixture.
2. Add spring onion, parsley, olives, salt, pepper and capers. Mix these well.
3. Decorate with capers. The warm salad is ready to eat.

SALADS

MEDITERRANEAN CHICKPEA SALAD

| Preparation time: 20 minutes | Total time: 20 minutes | Serves: 4 to 6 |

Ingredients

2 cups of cooked chickpeas, drained and rinsed
1 cup of cherry tomatoes, halved
4 medjool dates, pitted and diced
3 small cucumbers, cut into quarters
3 ounces of goat cheese, cut into small squares
Few strips of Romano salad leaves, cut into thin strips
¼ cup finely chopped parsley

For dressing

2 tbsp of extra virgin olive oil
3 cloves of garlic, minced
1 tbsp of lemon zest
2 tbsp of lemon juice
1 tsp of cumin seeds, roasted and finely powdered
¾ tsp of sea salt
¼ tsp of finely ground black pepper

Method

1. In a large bowl, add chickpeas, cherry tomatoes, dates and cucumbers and toss them nicely.
2. Transfer to a bowl or platter. Add cheese and mix softly.
3. Sprinkle with Romano salad strips and chopped parsley.
4. If desired, add dressing and serve, or dressing can be served separately and can be added as per taste.
5. For the dressing, add all the ingredients to a small bowl and mix them nicely. Keep aside.

Special Note

1. The goat cheese, dates and toasted cumin seeds give this chickpea salad delightful, sweet, savoury and aromatic flavours. It keeps well if prepared in advance.

SALADS

EASY GREEK SALAD

Preparation time: 15 minutes   Total time: 15 minutes   Serves: 4 to 6

Ingredients

3 **small cucumbers,** cut into ½″ thin rounds
1 **red pepper,** cut into 1½″ thin strips
2 **cups of cherry tomatoes,** cut into halves
5 **ounces of feta cheese,** cut into ½″ cubes
⅓ **cup of red onions,** thinly sliced
⅓ **cup of pitted kalamata olives**
⅓ **cup of fresh mint leaves,** for decoration

For dressing

¼ **cup of extra virgin olive oil**
1 **clove of garlic,** minced
½ **tsp of dried oregano,** more for sprinkling
¼ **tsp of Dijon mustard**
3 **tbsp of raw organic apple cider vinegar**
½ **tsp of sea salt**
¼ **tsp of finely ground black pepper**

Method

1. In a large bowl, add cucumbers, pepper, cherry tomatoes, feta cheese, onions and kalamata olives and toss them nicely.
2. Sprinkle with mint leaves.
3. If desired, add dressing and serve, or dressing can be served separately and can be added as per taste.
4. For the dressing, add all the ingredients to a small bowl and set aside.

Special Note

1. Dijon mustard and organic apple cider vinegar give this salad aromatic flavours. It keeps well if prepared in advance.

SALADS

RADICCHIO AND FRUIT SALAD

Preparation time: 20 minutes   Total time: 20 minutes   Serves: 4

Ingredients

1 small radicchio, finely sliced into small pieces
2 firm pears, sliced into thin wedges
1 big orange, cut into small pieces
75 g of walnut pieces
8 dates, pitted and finely chopped

For dressing

2 tbsp of agave syrup or honey
4 tbsp of olive oil
1 tsp of Dijon mustard
Zest of half an orange
½ tsp of rock salt, more can be added as per taste
¼ tsp of finely ground pepper
¼ tsp of finely ground cinnamon

Method

1. Take a medium-sized bowl and add radicchio, pears, orange pieces, walnut pieces and dates and mix these nicely.
2. For making the dressing, take a large bowl, add agave syrup, olive oil, mustard, zest of an orange, salt, pepper and cinnamon and whisk together.
3. Add the dressing to the radicchio and fruit mixture and combine it thoroughly.
4. Taste and add more salt if needed.

Special Notes

1. Deep burgundy-coloured radicchio goes well with sweet and ripe fruit as an elegant winter salad.
2. Persimmons can also be used instead of pears.

SALADS

SAMPHIRE, NEW POTATOES, BLACK BEANS AND FETA CHEESE

| Preparation time: 15 minutes | Cooking time: 20 minutes | Total time: 35 minutes | Serves: 4 |

Ingredients

250 g of cherry tomatoes, cut into halves
400 g of new potatoes
400 g of black beans, boiled, **or a can of beans** can also be used
100 g of samphire
50 g of salad leaves
75 g of feta

For dressing

3 tbsps of olive oil
1 clove of garlic, finely crushed finely
10 g of basil leaves, chopped
10 g of dill, chopped
1 tbsp of Dijon mustard, more can be added as per taste
Juice of one lemon
1 tsp of rock salt
¼ tsp of finely ground pepper

Method

1. Preheat the oven to 200 °C/gas 6. Halve the tomatoes and lay them cut-side up on a baking tray. Season with half of the salt and pepper and a little olive oil, approximately 1 tbsp, leaving the rest for dressing. Roast these for 10 to 15 minutes, until they are softened and start to blister. Remove and set aside.
2. Cut the potatoes in half if they are smaller in size, but if bigger, cut them into 3 pieces. Make sure that the pieces are of the same size. Take a pan, add water and put it on high heat to bring it to a boil. When boiling, add potatoes. Boil these until tender to the point of a knife (approx. 12–15 minutes). Leave them to drain in a colander.
3. Leave the samphire in a bowl of cold water to let the grit sink to the bottom for a couple of minutes. Then give it a quick rinse. Add a little water in another saucepan and let it boil. Add the samphire for 30 seconds. Drain and set aside. You can spread these on kitchen paper.
4. For the dressing, take a small bowl. Add the remaining olive oil, garlic, half of the basil and dill, mustard, lemon juice, salt and pepper.
5. Take a medium-sized bowl. Add beans and add half of the dressing and combine these nicely. Keep the other half for serving.
6. Take a serving platter and place salad leaves, potatoes, beans, tomatoes and samphire. Top with crumbled feta and remaining chopped basil and dill.

SALADS
ROASTED BROCCOLI, COURGETTE AND CHICKPEAS

Preparation time: 20 minutes Cooking time: 25 minutes Total time: 45 minutes Serves: 6

Ingredients

150 g of broccoli, cut into small florets; any large stems should be cut into small pieces
2 courgettes, cut in half, then cut into 1 cm thick slices
2 cloves of garlic, peeled and finely chopped
2 tbsp of olive oil
¾ tsp of rock salt, more can be added as per taste
½ tsp of finely ground pepper
1 tsp of ground cumin
¼ tsp of ground turmeric
¼ tsp of red chilli flakes (optional)
125 g of cherry tomatoes, halved
1 can of chickpeas, drained and patted dry with kitchen paper
30 g of pine nuts
150 g of baby spinach

For dressing

2 tbsp of tahini
Juice of 1 lemon
15 g of parsley, chopped coarsely
Few large mint leaves
A couple of tablespoons of water if required

Method

1. Preheat the oven to 200°C/gas 6. Transfer the broccoli, courgette and garlic to the roasting tray or tin. Pour over oil, salt, cumin, turmeric and chilli flakes and combine so that the vegetables are coated nicely. Spread these in a single layer and roast for 12 to 15 minutes, tossing halfway through.
2. Add the chickpeas to the roasting tin along with the pine nuts and stir through. Roast for a further 4 to 5 minutes, until the vegetables are tender and chickpeas have warmed through.
3. For the dressing, take a small bowl, add tahini, lemon juice, a little salt and half of the parsley and mint leaves.
4. Transfer the cooked vegetables to a bowl and combine them with tomatoes, remaining herbs and spinach leaves. These leaves may wilt slightly, which is fine.
5. Before serving, dressing should be poured over the vegetables.

SALADS

CAULIFLOWER, BUTTER BEANS AND KALE

| Preparation time: 15 minutes | Cooking time: 15 minutes | Total time: 30 minutes | Serves: 4 |

Ingredients

1 cauliflower, cut into small florets
200 g of frozen butter beans, defrosted
100 g of kale, roughly chopped into small pieces
A small bunch of flat leaf parsley, roughly chopped

For dressing

1 tbsp of capers, drained
1 tsp of Dijon mustard
1 to 2 tbsp of raw organic apple cider vinegar
½ tsp of rock salt, more can be added as per taste
¼ tsp of finely ground black pepper

Method

1. Put the cauliflower florets in a steamer and steam for 6 to 8 minutes or until tender. Keep them aside to cool.
2. Keep the frying pan over medium heat, add beans and let them cook for 2 to 3 minutes until they are little bit softer. Once they are soft, mix them with the florets.
3. Take a medium-sized pan and add enough water so that the kale is fully covered and let it boil. As soon as the water is boiling, add kale and let it boil for 2 minutes. Drain immediately and spread the kale on a cloth so that most of the water is squeezed out. Mix it with cauliflower and beans, taking care that the florets do not break. Add parsley and gently mix again.
4. For the dressing, take a medium-sized bowl. Add capers, mustard, vinegar, salt and pepper and mix them well.
5. Mix the dressing with florets, beans and kale mixture and combine properly.
6. Taste and add more salt and pepper if needed.

RICE & RICE-BASED

RICE & RICE-BASED

VEGETABLE AND PANEER BIRYANI

| Preparation time: 15 minutes | Cooking time: 35 minutes | Total time: 50 minutes | Serves: 6 to 8 |

Ingredients

2 cups of basmati rice
¼ medium broccoli broken into small florets
¼ medium cauliflower, broken into small florets
1 red pepper cut into 1″ pieces
100 g of cashew nuts (kaju)
250 g of paneer, cut into small cubes
3½ cups of water

Masala or tadka

3 tbsp of ghee (sunflower oil can also be used to make it **vegan**). I prefer ghee
4 pieces of clove
2 pieces of brown cardamom
3 pieces of bay leaf
1½ tsp of cumin seeds
1 tsp of black mustard seeds
½ tsp of asafoetida (hing powder)
1 tbsp of dry fenugreek (methi)
1 large onion, 4 cloves of garlic, 1½″ ginger, chopped in a food processor or cut into small pieces
1 tsp of turmeric powder
2 tsp of fine rock salt, more can be added as per taste
½ a can of 250 g of chopped tomato or 3 medium-sized fresh tomatoes, added into boiling water, peeled and chopped
1 tbsp of tomato puree
1 tbsp of lemon juice
1 green chilli, cut into small pieces or **⅓ tsp of red flaked chilli powder** (optional)
⅓ tsp of garam masala, finely ground
1 small bunch of coriander, cut roughly into small pieces. Add ½ while cooking and keep ½ aside for decoration

Method

1. Take a large heavy-based pan and keep on medium heat. Add ghee, and as soon as it gets a little hot, add cloves, cardamom and bay leaves along with cumin and mustard seeds. As soon as it starts bubbling (these should not be burnt), add methi leaves and soon after add the chopped mixture of onion, ginger and garlic.
2. When the mixture changes its colour to light pink, which may take 5 to 7 minutes, add turmeric and salt. After 2 to 3 minutes, add chopped tomato and tomato puree, and mix nicely. At this point, reduce the heat to low and cover the pan so that the tomatoes combine properly and turn into a smooth paste. This may take another 5 to 7 minutes. Check occasionally to ensure it is not burnt.
3. Add paneer and kaju pieces and mix them nicely with the paste. Leave this on the heat for a further 2 to 3 minutes. Add all the cut vegetables, half the coriander, and lemon juice, and combine them. Reduce the heat to low/medium and leave it on the heat for a further 7 to 8 minutes stirring occasionally. Add washed rice (rice should be washed only a few minutes before it is required and drained in a colander) and combine everything nicely.
4. When everything seems to be properly mixed, add water and turn the heat to high. As soon as it starts boiling, reduce the heat to the lowest temperature and cover the pan.

5. In general, the rice is not stirred while cooking, but as biryani has paneer and vegetables, there is a possibility that it can stick to the base of the pan. To avoid this, it is important that it is stirred properly, turning from top to bottom after 7 to 8 minutes of bringing it to a lower heat.
6. Normally, cooked rice has holes on top, but in biryani, the holes are not visible. After a few minutes, check if the rice is soft by pressing a few grains with your fingers. If they are soft, the biryani is ready. Sprinkle garam masala on top, cover, let it sit for a few minutes to allow the aroma to remain inside the biryani. Garnish with coriander before serving.

Biryani is normally eaten with plain yogurt or raita.

RICE & RICE-BASED

JEERA RICE

| Preparation time: 5 minutes | Cooking time: 20 minutes | Total time: 25 minutes | Servings: 4 to 6 |

Ingredients

1½ **cups of basmati rice,** washed
2¾ **cups of water**
1 **tsp of rock salt**
2 **tbsp of ghee or oil** of your choice
1 **tsp of cumin seeds/jeera seeds**
1 **bay leaf**
2 **brown cardamoms**
1 **cinnamon stick**

Method

1. Wash the rice 3 times in cold water and set aside.
2. Place a large saucepan on medium heat and add ghee. Add cumin seeds, bay leaf, cinnamon and cardamom pods, and gently fry for a few minutes.
3. Add rice and mix it nicely. Fry for another 1 to 2 minutes until the water seems to have evaporated.
4. Add water and increase the heat to high and let it boil. As soon as it starts boiling, reduce the heat to the lowest setting and cover the pan.
5. Rice is ready in 15 to 20 minutes. After 15 minutes, take out a few grains and press them with your fingers to check if they are done and there is no water. One tip to check if the rice has been cooked is that holes can be seen on the top.
6. Once done, transfer the jeera rice to a serving plate and fluff it with a fork and serve while hot.

Special Notes

1. Rice tastes best when served with rajma, chole, paneer sabz bahar and dal makhni, to name a few.
2. To make it **vegan** any oil can be used in place of butter.

RICE & RICE-BASED

PLAIN RICE

Preparation time: 5 minutes   Cooking time: 15 minutes   Total time: 20 minutes   Serves: 4

Ingredients

1 cup of basmati rice, washed
2 cups of water
¾ tsp of rock salt
1 tbsp of ghee (optional)
Few basil leaves

Method

1. Wash the rice 3 times in cold water and set aside.
2. Place a large saucepan on medium heat and add rice, water and salt and let it boil.
3. As soon as it starts boiling, add ghee and stir it so that it mixes well with the mixture.
4. Reduce the heat to low and cover the pan.
5. Rice is ready in 15 minutes. After 15 minutes, take out a few grains and press them with your fingers to check if they are done and there is no water. One tip to check if the rice has been cooked is that holes can be seen on the top.
6. If not ready, leave it for another few minutes.
7. Transfer rice to a serving plate and fluff it with a fork. Garnish with some basil leaves and serve while hot.
8. To make it **vegan**, olive oil can be used instead of ghee.

Special Note

1. Rice tastes best when served with rajma, chole, paneer sabz bahar and dal makhni, to name a few.

RICE & RICE-BASED

BROWN RICE

| Preparation time: 5 minutes | Cooking time: 35 minutes | Total time: 40 minutes | Serves: 4 to 6 |

Ingredients

1 cup of brown basmati rice, washed
2 cups of water
¾ tsp of rock salt
¼ tsp of haldi (turmeric)
1 tbsp of ghee or any oil of your choice
Few coriander leaves, cut coarsely

Method

1. Wash the rice 3 times in cold water and set aside.
2. Place a large saucepan on medium heat and add rice, salt, haldi and ghee and leave it to boil.
3. As soon as it starts boiling, stir it nicely, reduce the heat to low and cover the pan.
4. Rice is ready in 30 minutes. After 30 minutes, take out a few grains and press them with your fingers to check if they are done and there is no water. One tip to check if the rice has been cooked is that holes can be seen on the top.
5. If not ready, leave it for a few more minutes.
6. Transfer rice to a serving plate and fluff it with a fork. Garnish with coriander leaves and serve while hot.
7. To make it **vegan**, olive oil can be used instead of ghee.

Special Note

1. Rice tastes best when served with rajma, chole, paneer sabz bahar and dal makhni to name a few.

RICE & RICE-BASED

MATAR PULAO

Preparation time: 5 minutes   Cooking time: 25 minutes   Total time: 30 minutes   Serves: 4

Ingredients

200 g / 1 cup of basmati rice
200 g / 1½ cup of green peas (I use frozen peas)
1¾ cups of water

Masala or tadka

2 tbsp of butter or any oil of your choice
1 tsp of cumin seeds
3 brown cardamom pods
2 bay leaves
2 small cinnamon sticks
1 onion, thinly sliced
¾ tsp of rock salt

For decoration

10 cashews, lightly browned
Few coriander sprigs (optional)

Method

1. Wash the rice 3 times in cold water and set aside.
2. Place a large saucepan on medium heat and add butter.
3. As soon as it melts, add cumin seeds, cardamom pods, bay leaves, cinnamon sticks and stir it for a minute.
4. Add the onion and stir nicely. As soon as the colour of onion changes to light pink, add salt, and soon after, add the rice and stir until the water evaporates and the rice starts to look slightly transparent.
5. Add peas and mix them nicely.
6. Add water and bring it to a boil.
7. Once boiled, stir with a spatula, reduce the heat to the lowest temperature and cover the pan.
8. After the heat is reduced, it generally takes approximately 15 minutes to be ready.
9. After 15 minutes, take out a few grains of rice and press with your fingers to check if they are done. One tip to check if the rice is cooked is that you can see holes on the top once it is cooked.
10. Transfer rice to a serving plate and fluff it with a fork. Garnish with cashews and coriander leaves.
11. Serve while it is still hot.

Special Notes

1. Rice tastes best when served with rajma, chole, paneer sabz bahar and dal makhni, to name a few.
2. To make it **vegan**, any oil can be used in place of butter.

RICE & RICE-BASED

RED RICE

Preparation time: 5 minutes Cooking time: 50 minutes Total time: 55 minutes Serves: 4

Red rice is diabetic-friendly. This is based on my own experience.
I am sharing how to cook whole grain red rice in two different ways. The first option is to make it in a pressure cooker, and the second option is to make it in a pan.

Ingredients

1 cup of red rice
2 cups of water
¾ tsp of rock salt
1 tbsp of ghee or any oil of your choice

Method

OPTION 1

1. Wash the rice 3 times and soak it overnight in a big bowl of water.
2. In the morning, drain the water and add the rice to the pressure cooker.
3. Keep the pressure cooker on high heat. Add water, salt and ghee or oil as preferred. Stir to mix and close the lid with the pressure valve. Let it whistle at least 5 to 6 times.
4. Open the lid when the pressure is released. Check if the rice has become soft and if there is no water.
5. If there is water, close the pressure cooker again and cook for 2 or 3 more whistles.
6. Repeat the same process and, if ready, fluff it with a fork and transfer it into a shallow platter.
7. It is best if eaten when hot.

OPTION 2

1. If following the second option, there is no need to soak the water overnight.
2. Wash the rice 3 times and add it to the heavy-based pan.
3. Keep the pan on high heat, add water, salt and ghee or oil.
4. Mix it and leave it to boil.
5. As soon as it starts boiling, bring the heat to the lowest setting, cover with the lid and let it boil for 40 to 45 minutes.
6. Open the lid after 45 minutes and check if the rice has become soft and if there is no water left.
7. If there is any water, cover the pan and keep it for another 5 minutes or until the rice has become soft.
8. Transfer into a serving plate and fluff it with a fork, decorate with coriander leaves and serve while hot.

Special Notes

1. This tastes best when served with rajma, chole, paneer sabz bahar, dal makhni or any dry vegetable, to name a few.
2. If eaten with dry vegetables, homemade yogurt or any yogurt can be eaten with them.
3. To make it **vegan**, olive oil can be used instead of ghee.

RICE & RICE-BASED

CHAPATIS

CHAPATIS

WHEAT CHAPATIS

| Preparation time: 5 minutes | Cooking time: 20 minutes | Total time: 25 minutes | Makes: 8 chapatis |

Ingredients

200 g of wholemeal wheat flour
50 g of flour for dusting
150 ml of lukewarm water
1 tbsp of olive oil

Method

1. In a large bowl, add the flour and olive oil and stir it nicely with a wooden spoon. Add enough water to make a soft dough that is elastic but not sticky. Knead it for 2 to 3 minutes until it is smooth. Chapatis come out better if kept for half an hour after kneading. Divide into 8 pieces or more if you want to make them smaller. Roll each piece into a ball. Keep them aside.
2. Heat an iron tawa or frying pan on medium heat until it is hot. It can be greased lightly or can be left as it is. On a lightly floured surface, use a floured rolling pin to roll out the balls of dough until they become very thin.
3. When the pan starts smoking, put one chapati on it. Cook until the underside has light brown spots or has changed its colour, about 30 seconds, then flip and cook the other side. At this point, the chapati can be kept directly on the fire to do the final cooking or left on the pan and flipped once more.
4. Put on a plate and keep warm while you cook the rest of the chapatis.

Special Note

1. Chapatis can be served with rajma, chole, paneer sabz bahar and dal makhni, to name a few.

CHAPATIS

JOWAR (SORGHUM) ROTI (CHAPATI)

| Preparation time: 5 minutes | Cooking time: 20 minutes | Total time: 25 minutes | Makes: 8 chapatis |

Ingredients

150 g of jowar flour
50 g of wheat flour
50 g of flour for dusting
150 ml of lukewarm water
1 tbsp of olive oil

Method

1. In a large bowl, add both the flours and olive oil and stir them nicely with a wooden spoon. Add enough water to make a soft dough that is elastic but not sticky. Knead it for 2 to 3 minutes until it is smooth. Chapatis will come out better if kept for half an hour after kneading. Divide into 8 pieces or more if you want to make these smaller. Roll each piece into a ball. Keep it aside.
2. Heat an iron tawa or a heavy-based frying pan on medium heat until it is hot. It can be greased lightly or left as it is. On a lightly floured surface, use a floured rolling pin to roll out the balls of dough. This flour is not very sticky; therefore, these should be rolled softly. Try to roll it carefully so that it does not break.
3. When the pan starts smoking, place one chapati on it. Cook until the underside develops light brown spots or changes colour, about 30 seconds, then flip and cook the other side. At this point, you can either place the chapati

directly on the flame for final cooking or leave it on the pan, flipping once or twice more.
4. Put on a plate and keep warm while you cook the rest of them.

Special Notes

1. Chapatis can be served with rajma, chole, paneer sabz bahar and dal makhni, to name a few.
2. Jowar is good for people who have diabetes.

CHUTNEYS & RAITA

CHUTNEYS & RAITA

YOGURT AND MINT CHUTNEY

Preparation time: 10 minutes | Total time: 10 minutes | Makes a big bowl

Ingredients

500 g of thick yogurt
20 mint leaves, chopped finely in a small grinder
2 tbsp of desiccated coconut
¾ tsp of rock salt, more can be added as per taste
¼ tsp of black pepper
¼ tsp of flaked red pepper
1 tbsp of virgin olive oil (optional)
1 tbsp of lemon juice (optional)

Method

1. Beat the yogurt with a whisk to remove any lumps.
2. Add the chopped mint and all other ingredients, and combine completely.
3. Remove the chutney into a bowl and keep it aside.

Special Note

1. Yogurt and mint chutney can be eaten with Handwa, besan puda, any type of pakoras or any other savoury snacks.

CHUTNEYS & RAITA

GREEN MANGO CHUTNEY

Preparation time: 20 minutes | Total time: 20 minutes | Makes a big bowl

Ingredients

1 bunch of coriander or 100 g, washed and cut coarsely
4 sprigs of mint, leaves separated, washed
3 small raw mangoes, cut into small pieces
1 medium onion, cut into small pieces
2″ ginger, cut into small pieces
3 green chillies, cut into small pieces
¼ rind of unwaxed lemon, cut into small pieces
¾ tsp of rock salt, more can added as per taste
½ tsp of haldi powder
1 tsp of ground cumin seed powder
1 tsp of ground coriander powder
1 tbsp of lemon juice
2 tbsp of water, if required

Method

1. Add all the above ingredients to a food processor and make a smooth paste.
2. Add 1 or 2 tbsp of water if the paste seems thick. But don't make the chutney too thin or watery.
3. Remove the chutney from the bowl and set it aside.

Special Note

1. Green mango chutney can be eaten with Handwa, besan puda, any type of pakoras or any other savoury snacks.

CHUTNEYS & RAITA

IMLI KI CHUTNEY OR TAMARIND CHUTNEY

| Preparation time: 10 minutes | Cooking time: 20 minutes | Total time: 30 minutes | Makes a big bowl |

Ingredients

250 g of soft tamarind (imli)
2 cups of sugar or gur (jaggery)
½ cup of water, more can be added if required
1 tsp of rock salt, more can be added as per taste
½ tsp of red chilli flakes
1″ ginger piece
1 tbsp of cumin (jeera) seeds
2 tsp of melon seeds (optional)

Method

1. Dry roast the cumin seeds in a frying pan until they turn brown. When they get cold, these should be coarsely ground.
2. Soak the imli in lukewarm water so that it softens. More can be added if required.
3. Rub well to remove the seeds.
4. Strain all the juice into a container.
5. Put on a low heat and bring the juice to a boil.
6. Add gur or sugar, salt, chilli powder and roasted jeera seeds, and keep stirring. Let it simmer on low heat until it starts to become thick.
7. Ginger can be added as a whole for flavour while it is simmering and can be removed after a few minutes.
8. When the desired consistency is reached, remove from the heat and allow it to completely cool.
9. Half of the melon seeds are to be added to the chutney, and remaining to be used for decoration.

Special Note

1. Imli chutney can be eaten with Handwa, besan puda, any types of pakoras or any other savoury snacks.

CHUTNEYS & RAITA

SEARED GINGER RAITA

Preparation time: 10 minutes   Cooking time: 5 minutes   Total time: 15 minutes   Makes a medium-sized bowl

Ingredients

1½ **cups of plain yogurt,** any level of fat
¼ **cup of ginger,** finely chopped
1 **tbsp of chopped mint leaves**
¼ **cup of ginger,** finely julienned
½ **to 1 tsp of rock salt,** as per taste
1 **tbsp of olive oil**
½ **tsp of black or brown mustard seeds**
2 **fresh red or green chillies**
20 **curry leaves**

Method

1. Put the yogurt into a large bowl and whisk it a few times to break it up. Add the chopped ginger, mint leaves and salt to taste.
2. In a small skillet, heat the oil over medium-high heat. Add curry leaves and as they become dark, add julienned ginger. Raise the heat to high and continue stirring constantly until the ginger starts turning brown and caramelising. Now add mustard seeds.
3. When mustard seeds start popping, add chillies and switch off the heat.
4. Pour the mixture into the yogurt, leaving some for decoration, and stir to combine.
5. Decorate with the remaining mixture.

Special Note

1. Seared ginger raita can be eaten with Handwa, besan puda, any type of pakoras or any other savoury snacks.

SET LUNCH & DINNER MENU

SET LUNCH & DINNER MENU

VEGETABLE AND PANEER BIRYANI

| Preparation time: 15 minutes | Cooking time: 35 minutes | Total time: 50 minutes | Serves: 6 to 8 |

Ingredients

2 cups of basmati rice
¼ medium broccoli broken into small florets
¼ medium cauliflower broken into small florets
1 red pepper cut into 1″ pieces
100 g of cashew nuts (kaju)
250 g of paneer, cut into small cubes
3½ cups of water

Masala or tadka

3 tbsp of ghee (sunflower oil can also be used to make it **vegan**). I prefer ghee
4 pieces of cloves
2 pieces of brown cardamom
3 pieces of bay leaf
1½ tsp of cumin seeds
1 tsp of black mustard seeds
½ tsp of asafoetida (hing powder)
1 tbsp of dry fenugreek (methi)
1 large onion, 4 cloves of garlic, 1½″ ginger, chopped in a food processor or cut into small pieces
1 tsp of turmeric powder
2 tsp of fine rock salt, more can be added as per taste
½ a can of 250 g of chopped tomato or 3 medium-sized fresh tomatoes, added into boiling water, peeled and chopped
1 tbsp of tomato puree
1 green chilli, cut into small pieces or **⅓ tsp of red flaked chilli powder** (optional)
⅓ tsp of garam masala, finely ground
1 small bunch of coriander cut roughly into small pieces. Add ½ while cooking and keep ½ to be kept aside for decoration

Method

1. Take a large heavy-based pan and keep on medium heat. Add ghee, and as soon as it gets a little hot, add cloves, cardamom and bay leaves along with cumin and mustard seeds. Once it starts bubbling (these should not be burnt), add methi leaves and soon after add the chopped mixture of onion, ginger and garlic.
2. When the mixture changes its colour to light pink, which may take 5 to 7 minutes, add turmeric and salt. After 2 to 3 minutes, add chopped tomato and tomato puree, and mix nicely. At this point, reduce the heat to low and cover the pan so that the tomatoes combine properly and turn into a smooth paste. This may take another 5 to 7 minutes. Check occasionally to ensure it is not burnt.
3. Add paneer and kaju pieces and mix them nicely with the paste. Leave this on the heat for a further 2 to 3 minutes. Add all the cut vegetables, half the coriander, and lemon juice, and combine them. Reduce the heat to low/medium and leave it on the heat for a further 7 to 8 minutes stirring occasionally. Add washed rice (the rice should be washed only a few minutes before it is required and drained in a colander) and combine everything nicely.
4. When everything seems to be properly mixed, add water and turn the heat to high. As soon as it starts boiling, reduce the heat to the lowest temperature and cover the pan.
5. In general, the rice is not stirred while cooking, but as biryani has paneer and vegetables, there is a possibility that it can stick to the base of the pan. To avoid this, it is important that it is stirred properly, turning from top to bottom after 7 to 8 minutes of bringing it to a lower heat.

SET LUNCH & DINNER MENU

6. Normally, cooked rice has holes on top, but in biryani, they aren't visible. After a few minutes, check if the rice is soft by pressing a few grains with your fingers. If they are soft, the biryani is ready. Sprinkle garam masala on top, cover and let it sit for a few minutes to trap the aroma. Garnish with coriander before serving.

Biryani is normally eaten with plain yogurt or raita.

SET LUNCH & DINNER MENU

PASTA WITH COURGETTE AND MUSHROOM

Preparation time: 15 minutes | Cooking time: 25 minutes | Total time: 40 minutes | Serves: 4

Ingredients

300 g of pasta
2 medium-sized courgettes, cut into half, then quartered and cut into ½″ pieces
200 g of button mushrooms, smaller ones can be left whole, bigger ones to be cut into halves or quarters depending on size
1 medium-sized onion, cut into small pieces
4 cloves of garlic, cut into small pieces
200 g of chopped tomatoes or 4 fresh tomatoes, cut into small pieces
1 tsp of tomato puree
1 red chilli, cut into small pieces (optional)
4 tbsp of olive oil
½ tsp of basil or oregano herbs
¼ tsp of black pepper, finely ground
¾ tsp of rock salt
200 g of grated mozzarella (optional)
Few sprigs of spring onion, cut into small pieces, to be used for garnishing

Method

1. Take a heavy pan and keep it on medium heat. Add oil, leaving 1 tbsp aside. As soon as it gets a little hot, add onion and garlic pieces. Leave these for a minute or so until they turn light pink.
2. Add tomato, tomato puree, herbs and salt. Mix these properly and cover the pan. The heat can be reduced to low and left for 7 to 8 minutes. These should be thoroughly mixed.
3. Add courgette, mushroom and chilli if used, and stir these so that they are covered properly with the onion and tomato mixture. The pan should be covered and left on the heat for 10 minutes or until the courgette becomes soft.
4. At the same time, take a large pan, add water and bring it to a boil.
5. Add a little salt and oil. As soon as the water starts boiling, add the pasta. Let it boil as per the instructions given on the packet. Once they become soft to the touch or as preferred, the water should be drained. Courgette/mushroom sauce should be mixed with the pasta.
6. This should be transferred to a large bowl, sprinkled with pepper on top and decorated with spring onion.

Special Note

1. Another option is to sprinkle some grated mozzarella cheese on top of pasta and grill it on high settings for 5 minutes or until the cheese turns a little brown. The cheese-baked pasta is ready.

SET LUNCH & DINNER MENU

SET LUNCH & DINNER MENU

POTATO, COURGETTE AND SALAD

Preparation time: 75 minutes   Total time: 75 minutes   Serves: 4

Crispy thyme potatoes

600 g or 6 red potatoes, thinly sliced
50 g of melted butter
1 tsp of rock salt, more can be added as per taste
¾ tsp of black pepper, finely ground
2 tbsp of thyme, only the leaves
Few sprigs of thyme for decoration

Method

1. Heat the oven to 220 °C. I use the oven with a fan option, and it works well. Take a large shallow baking dish. Add potatoes, butter, salt, pepper and thyme leaves.
2. Combine these nicely and keep them in the preheated oven. Potatoes will come out crispy if all the pieces are nicely spread out.
3. Keep it in the oven for 20 minutes. Before taking it out, it is important to check if the potato pieces have softened, turned brownish and crispy.
4. Garnish with sprigs of thyme.

Baked courgette with cheese

3 courgettes, cut into small disc-like round pieces
1 large onion, cut into thin long pieces
¼ tsp of turmeric powder
¾ tsp of fine rock salt, more can be added as per taste
½ tsp of black pepper, finely ground
⅓ tsp of dried basil or oregano herb
¼ tsp of flaked red chilli (optional)
3 to 4 tbsp of extra virgin olive oil
120 g of mozzarella cheese, grated

Method

1. Courgette can be cooked together with potatoes in the oven at the same time.
2. Take a large shallow baking dish and add courgette and onion pieces. Add turmeric, salt, pepper, herb, chilli powder (if using) and oil and mix these nicely. The dish will come out good if all the pieces are nicely spread out before putting in the oven.
3. Keep in the oven for 20 minutes. Before taking it out, it is important to check if the courgette pieces have softened and turned brownish. Spread the cheese evenly and put the dish back in the oven on high heat under the grill for 5 minutes or until the cheese has turned a light brownish colour.

Rocket salad with avocado and cherry tomatoes

100 g of rocket salad
2 medium avocados, cut into halves, then cut into thin slices
200 g of cherry tomatoes, washed
2 tbsp of flaxseed oil
½ tsp of rock salt
¼ tsp of pepper
1 tbsp of milled organic flaxseed

Method

1. Take a medium-sized bowl. Add dried rocket leaves, then add salt, pepper and flaxseed and mix these properly.
2. Then add the oil and mix it again.
3. Once properly mixed, spread it on a large plate, then spread avocado pieces on top, and in the end, add cherry tomatoes.

The above menu can be offered for lunch or dinner.

Special Note

1. Potatoes and courgettes can be put in the oven at the same time.

SET LUNCH & DINNER MENU

SWEET POTATO AND VEGETABLE TIKKI (BURGER) WITH SORGHUM

Preparation time: 25 minutes   Cooking time: 20 minutes   Total time: 45 minutes   Serves: 4

INGREDIENTS

- **2 sweet potatoes or potatoes,** boiled, peeled and mashed or can be cut into small pieces
- **4 tbsp of sorghum or millet flour: 2 serving spoons** (both flours are beneficial for diabetics)
- **2 medium carrots,** grated
- **2 courgettes,** grated
- **1 large onion,** grated or cut into small pieces
- **2″ ginger,** grated
- **¼ unwaxed lemon rind,** cut into small pieces or grated
- **4 sprigs of parsley,** cut into small pieces
- **1 tsp of fine rock salt,** more can be added as per the taste
- **¾ tsp of turmeric powder**
- **½ tsp of cumin seeds,** finely ground
- **1 tsp of coriander seeds,** finely ground
- **1 tsp of sesame seeds**
- **1 small green chilli,** cut into small pieces (optional)
- **3 tbsp of coconut oil or any other oil** for frying

METHOD

1. Add all the ingredients except oil in a large bowl and combine them. Using hands for mixing ensures that all the ingredients are thoroughly combined.
2. Take a heavy-based pan and keep on low/medium heat. I use a heavy-bottom steel pan. Add ½ tbsp of oil and wait until it gets hot.
3. Take 2 tbsp from the mixture and flatten it into a burgerdisc in the palm of your hand, then place it on the pan. Depending on the size of the pan, you can put 2 or 3 at a time. After a couple of minutes, it should be turned to the other side with a flat and sharp spatula. These should be turned 2 to 3 times until both sides turn a brownish colour to your liking. As the mixture is very soft, special attention needs to be taken when turning.
4. 8 to 10 tikkis can be made with this mixture. These numbers can differ according to the size of the mixture used for each.

SPECIAL NOTE

1. Tikkis are eaten with salad, yogurt or chutney.
2. Gram flour can also be used instead of sorghum or millet flour.
3. Any leftover vegetables can also be used instead of carrots and courgettes.

SET LUNCH & DINNER MENU

RAJMA/KIDNEY BEANS CURRY AND JEERA RICE

| Preparation time: 15 minutes | Cooking time: 60 minutes | Total time: 75 minutes | Serves: 4 to 6 |

Rajma/kidney beans curry

To pressure-cook

1½ cups of raw kidney beans, approximately 300 g, soaked in four cups of lukewarm water. If required, raw beans can be replaced with **⅔ tins of red kidney beans, 400 g each**
3½ cups of water, approximately 28 oz
1 tsp of rock salt

For the masala

1 large onion, 4 cloves of garlic and 1½″ ginger, chopped in a food processor or cut into tiny pieces
1 green chilli, chopped or cut into small pieces (optional)
2 tbsp of ghee or any oil as per your choice
½″ of lemon rind, finely grated
2 tsp of tomato puree
½ a can of chopped tomatoes, approximately 250 g or **3 medium-sized tomatoes,** chopped in a food processor
1 tbsp of dry fenugreek leaves (methi)
½ tsp of turmeric powder
1 tsp of cumin seeds
½ tsp of black mustard seeds
1 tsp of coriander powder
1 tsp of rock salt, more can be added after tasting
1 tsp of garam masala
Few sprigs of fresh coriander cut into small pieces, coarsely

Method

1. Wash the beans at least 3 times and then soak them overnight in approximately 4 cups of lukewarm water. In the morning, drain the water in which the beans were soaked and then transfer them to a pressure cooker. Add 3½ cups of fresh water and 1 tsp of salt.
2. Place the pressure cooker on high heat for 4 whistles. Let the pressure release naturally. Beans should be completely soft at this point.
3. Take a large heavy-bottomed pan and keep on medium heat. Add ghee or oil of your choice. When the ghee gets a little hot, add cumin and mustard seeds. As soon as they start bubbling, add the mixture of onion, ginger and garlic and cook these for 7 to 8 minutes, stirring often. Once the colour changes to light brown, add turmeric, salt, coriander powder and fenugreek leaves. Then add chopped tomato, tomato puree and chilli and mix these nicely. At this point, reduce the heat to low and cover the pan so that the tomatoes combine properly and turn into a smooth paste. This takes 8 to 10 minutes. This paste should be stirred occasionally so that it does not burn.
4. Add the boiled beans along with the water in which they were boiled. Mix these properly and let them simmer for 20 to 30 minutes. While these are simmering, take some of the beans out of the pan and mash them with a potato masher, then mix these again with the rest of the bean curry. This makes the curry creamier and thickens it.
5. If the consistency seems quite thick, a few tablespoons of water can be added as per your preference.
6. Half of the coriander leaves should be added while the curry is still simmering.
7. Finally, switch off the heat and sprinkle garam masala, and cover it so that the flavour is retained.
8. Sprinkle fresh coriander before serving.

SET LUNCH & DINNER MENU

Jeera rice

- 1½ **cups of basmati rice,** washed
- 2¾ **cups of water**
- **1 tsp of rock salt**
- **2 tbsp of ghee or oil** of your choice
- **1 tsp of cumin seeds/jeera seeds**
- **1 bay leaf**
- **2 brown cardamoms**
- **1 cinnamon stick**

Method

1. Wash the rice 3 times in cold water and set aside.
2. Place a large saucepan on medium heat and add ghee. Add cumin seeds, bay leaf, cinnamon and cardamom pods and gently fry for a few minutes.
3. Add rice and mix it nicely. Fry for another 1 to 2 minutes until the water seems to have evaporated.
4. Add water and increase the heat to high and let it boil. As soon as it starts boiling, reduce the heat to the lowest setting and cover the pan.
5. Rice is ready in 15 to 20 minutes. After 15 minutes, take out a few grains and press them with your fingers to check if they are done and there is no water. One tip to check if the rice has been cooked is that holes can be seen on the top.
6. Once done, transfer the jeera rice to a serving plate and fluff it with a fork, decorate with some finely chopped coriander leaves and serve while hot.

Special Note

1. Rajma/kidney bean curry and jeera rice go very well together and are a special favourite of children.

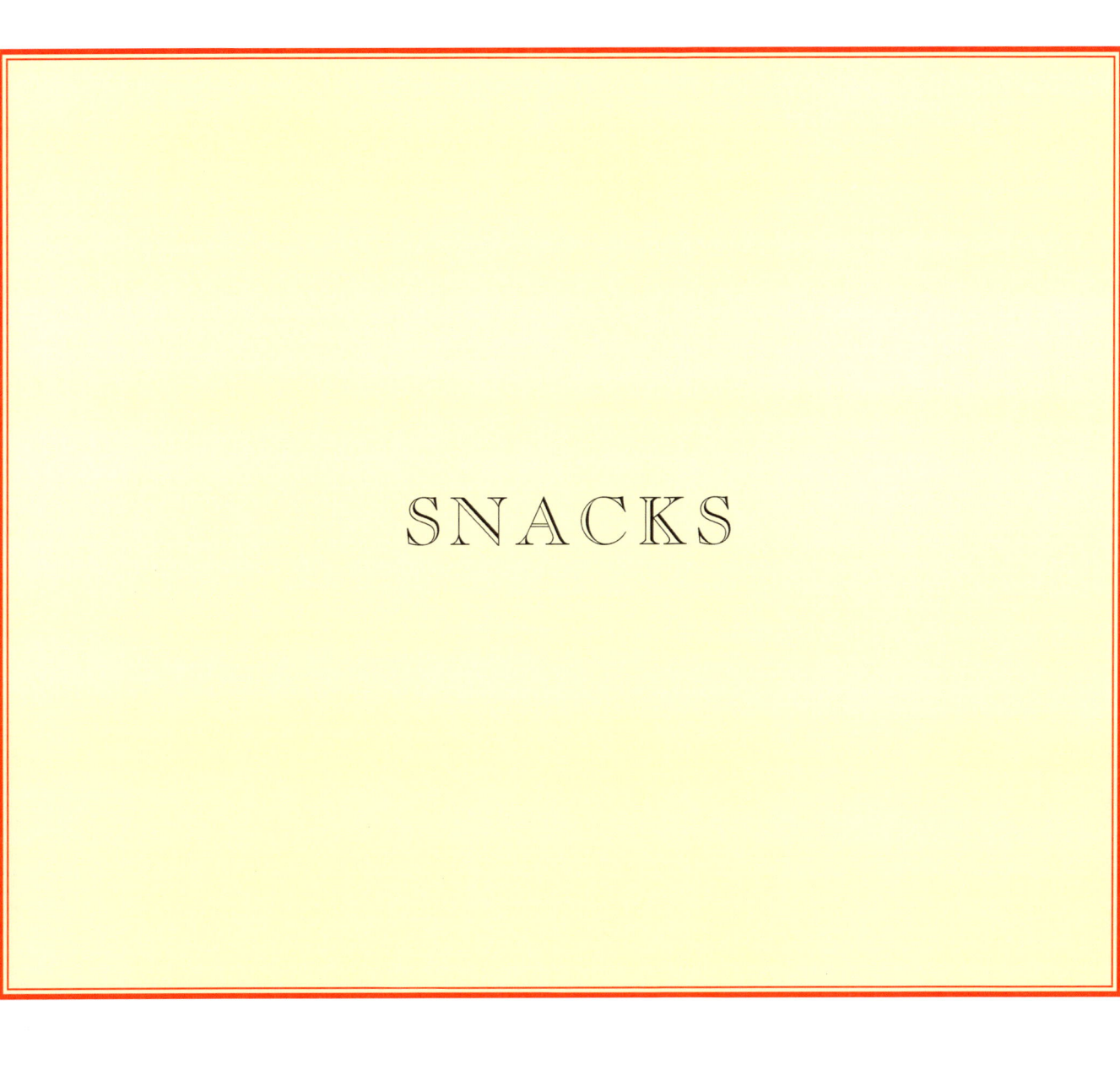

SAVOURY SNACKS

SAVOURY SNACKS

ALOO (POTATO) PAKORAS

| Preparation time: 10 minutes | Cooking time: 20 minutes | Total time: 30 minutes | Serves: 4 |

Ingredients

2 medium potatoes, peeled, cut into thin pieces (not too thin) and kept in water until used
100 g of besan (gram flour)
1″ ginger, grated
½ tsp of rock salt (or as required)
⅛ tsp of turmeric powder
¼ tsp of red chilli flakes (optional)
1 green chilli, crushed finely (optional)
1 tsp of dry methi
¼ tsp of ajwain seeds (carom seeds)
¼ tsp of baking powder (optional). This makes pakoras crisp
150 ml of water (can vary depending on the consistency required)
Oil for frying as required. Use **any neutral-flavoured oil** with a high smoking point to deep fry, such as **sunflower oil**
Chaat masala (optional)

Making batter

1. Take out the potato pieces from the water and keep them in a bowl. Add a little salt and a pinch of chilli powder and keep aside.
2. Take another medium-sized bowl, add gram flour, ginger, salt, turmeric powder, red and green chilli, methi, ajwain seeds and baking powder in a mixing bowl.
3. Add water and make it into a medium consistency. This should neither be too thick nor too thin.
4. Taste the batter and add more salt if required.

Deep fry

1. Take a deep kadai or pan and keep it on medium heat. The quantity of oil should be enough so that the potatoes are immersed completely.
2. While the oil heats, drain all the water from the potatoes completely.
3. Drop a little portion of the batter into the oil to see if the oil is hot enough. If the batter rises immediately without browning, it is the right temperature.
4. Dip each slice of potato in batter to coat these completely and then gently sliding these to the oil. The number of potatoes added at one time will depend on the size of the kadai and the quantity of oil. Do not stir for a few seconds, then start stirring so that they do not stick together.
5. When one size of pakoras firm up, look cooked and are light brown, turn it over gently and fry the other side.
6. Turn them over a couple of times and fry until crisp and golden.
7. Once done, remove them with a slotted spoon, draining as much oil as possible in the pan.
8. Place these on kitchen paper or in a steel colander.
9. Repeat making the next batches as above. Ensure the oil is not too hot at any time. Heat can be reduced a little anytime to keep the oil at the right temperature.
10. Serve these with any green or imli chutney and a cup of tea or coffee, and enjoy.

Special Note

1. Pakoras make for an excellent evening tea-time snack. These are served with green chutney, yogurt or imli chutney.

SAVOURY SNACKS

SAVOURY SNACKS

ONION PAKORAS

Preparation time: 10 minutes | Cooking time: 20 minutes | Total time: 30 minutes | Serves: 4

Ingredients

2 onions, finely sliced into rounded shape, soak in cold water
100 g of besan (gram flour)
1″ ginger, grated
¾ tsp of rock salt (or as per the taste)
⅛ tsp of turmeric powder
¼ tsp of red chilli flakes (optional)
1 green chilli, crushed finely (optional)
1 tsp of dry methi
¼ tsp of ajwain seeds (carom seeds)
¼ tsp of baking powder (optional). This makes it crisp
150 ml of water (can vary depending on the consistency required)
Oil for frying as required – use **any neutral-flavoured oil** with a high smoking point to deep fry, such as **sunflower oil**

Making batter

1. Take out the onion pieces from the water and keep them in a bowl. Add a little salt and a pinch of chilli powder and set aside.
2. Add gram flour, ginger, salt, red and green chilli, methi, turmeric powder, ajwain seeds and baking powder in a mixing bowl.
3. Add water slowly, little by little, and make into a medium consistency. It should neither be too thick nor too thin.
4. Taste the batter and add more salt if required.

Method

1. Take a deep kadai or pan and keep it on medium heat. The quantity of oil should be enough so that the onion pieces are immersed completely.
2. While the oil heats, drain all the water from the onions completely.
3. Drop a little portion of the batter into the oil to see if the oil is hot enough. If the batter rises immediately without browning, it is the right temperature.
4. Mix the onion pieces into the batter and coat them completely. Start gently sliding them into the oil. The quantity of onions added at one time will depend on the size of the kadai and the quantity of oil. Do not stir for a few seconds, then start stirring so that they do not stick together.
5. When one side of the pakoras firm up, look cooked and are light brown, turn them over gently and fry the other side.
6. Turn them over a couple of times and fry until crisp and golden.
7. Once done, remove them with a slotted spoon, draining as much oil as possible in the pan.
8. Place these on kitchen paper or in a steel colander.
9. Repeat making the next batches as above. Ensure the oil is not too hot at any time. Heat can be reduced a little anytime to keep the oil at the right temperature.
10. Serve these with any green or imli chutney and a cup of tea or coffee, and enjoy.

Special Note

1. Pakoras make for an excellent evening tea-time snack. These are served with green, yogurt or imli chutney.

SAVOURY SNACKS

SAVOURY SNACKS

AUBERGINE PAKORAS

Preparation time: 10 minutes   Cooking time: 20 minutes   Total time: 30 minutes   Serves: 4

Ingredients

1 large aubergine, cut into thin round pieces (not too thin) and kept in water until used
100 g of besan (gram flour)
1″ ginger, grated
½ tsp of rock salt (or as required)
⅛ tsp of turmeric powder
¼ tsp of red chilli flakes (optional)
1 green chilli (optional), crushed finely
1 tbsp of dry methi
¼ tsp of ajwain seeds (carom seeds)
½ tsp of baking powder (optional). This makes pakoras crisp
150 ml of water (can vary depending on the consistency required)
Oil for frying as required – use **any neutral-flavoured oil** with a high smoking point to deep fry, such as **sunflower oil**

Making batter

1. Take the aubergine pieces out of the water and keep them in a bowl. Add a little salt and a pinch of chilli powder and set aside.
2. Take another medium-sized bowl, add gram flour, ginger, salt, turmeric powder, red and green chilli, methi, ajwain seeds and baking powder, and mix these nicely.
3. Add water slowly, little by little, and make into a medium consistency. It should neither be too thick nor too thin.
4. Taste the batter and add more salt if required.

Deep fry

1. Take a deep kadai or pan and keep it on medium heat. The quantity of the oil should be enough so that the aubergine pieces are immersed completely.
2. While the oil heats, drain all the water from the aubergine pieces completely.
3. Drop a little portion of the batter into the oil to see if the oil is hot enough. If the batter rises immediately without browning, it is the right temperature.
4. Dip each aubergine piece in batter and coat it completely before gently sliding it into the oil. The number of these pieces added at one time will depend on the size of the kadai and the quantity of oil. Do not stir for a few seconds; then stir occasionally to prevent them from sticking together.
5. When one side of pakoras firm up, look cooked and are light brown, turn them over gently and fry the other side.
6. Turn them over a couple of times and fry them until crisp and golden.
7. Once done, remove them with a slotted spoon, draining as much oil as possible in the pan.
8. Place these on kitchen paper or in a steel colander.
9. Repeat making the next batch as above. Ensure the oil is not too hot at any time. Heat can be reduced a little at any time to keep the oil at the right temperature.
10. Serve these with any green or imli chutney and a cup of tea or coffee, and enjoy.

Special Note

1. Pakoras make for an excellent evening tea-time snack. These are served with green chutney, yogurt or imli chutney.

SAVOURY SNACKS

SAVOURY SNACKS

CAULIFLOWER PAKORAS

Preparation time: 10 minutes   Cooking time: 20 minutes   Total time: 30 minutes   Serves: 4

Ingredients

- ½ **medium-sized cauliflower** or **350 g** florets separated from the cauliflower, cut into 1″ pieces (not to be chopped to smaller than 1″); keep in hot water
- **Few spinach leaves** or **approximately 50 g**
- **100 g of besan (gram flour)**
- 1″ **ginger,** grated
- ½ **tsp of rock salt** (or as required)
- ½ **tsp of baking powder** (optional). This makes pakoras crisp
- ⅛ **tsp of turmeric powder**
- ¼ **tsp of red chilli flakes** (optional)
- 1 **green chilli,** crushed finely (optional)
- **1 tsp of dry methi**
- ¼ **tsp of ajwain seeds (carom seeds)**
- ½ **tsp of baking powder** (optional). This makes pakoras crisp
- **150 ml of water** (can vary depending on the consistency required)
- **Oil** for frying as required – use **any neutral-flavoured oil** with a high smoking point to deep fry, such as **sunflower oil**

Making batter

1. Take out the florets from the hot water after 1 or 2 minutes. This step is done to bring out the worms, if any in the florets.
2. Drain the water and transfer the florets to a bowl. Add a little salt and a pinch of chilli powder and keep aside.
3. Add gram flour, ginger, salt, baking powder, turmeric powder, red and green chilli, methi, ajwain seeds and spinach leaves in a mixing bowl.
4. Add water slowly, little by little, and make into a medium consistency. It should neither be too thick nor too thin.
5. Make sure that all florets are completely coated.
6. Taste the batter and add more salt if required.

Deep fry

1. Take a deep kadai or pan and keep on medium heat. The quantity of the oil should be enough so that the florets are immersed completely.
2. While the oil heats, drain all the water from the florets completely.
3. Drop a small portion of the batter into the oil to see if the oil is hot enough. If the batter rises immediately without browning, it is the right temperature.
4. Gently drop each floret separately in the hot oil. The quantity of florets that can be added at any one time will depend on the size of the kadai and the quantity of the oil. Do not crowd a lot of them as they will get stuck and won't fry well.
5. Do not stir for a few seconds, then start stirring so that they do not stick together.
6. When one side of the pakoras firm up, look cooked and are light brown, turn them gently and fry the other side.

7. Turn them over a couple of times and fry them until crisp and golden.
8. Once done, remove them with a slotted spoon, draining as much oil as possible in the pan.
9. Place these on kitchen paper or in a steel colander.
10. Repeat making the next batches as above. Ensure the oil is not too hot at any time. Heat can be reduced a little anytime to keep the oil at the right temperature.
11. Serve these with any green or imli chutney and a cup of tea or coffee, and enjoy.

Special Note

1. Pakoras make for an excellent evening tea-time snack. These are served with green, yogurt or imli chutney.

SAVOURY SNACKS

MIXED VEG PAKORA

| Preparation time: 30 minutes | Cooking time: 20 minutes | Total time: 50 minutes | Serves: 4 |

Vegetable mix preparation

- 2 medium-sized onions
- 3 medium-sized potatoes
- ¼ cauliflower
- 75 g of spinach leaves
- ¼ quarter lemon rind
- 1" **ginger,** grated
- 1 **green chilli** (more or less can be added as per taste)
- 1 tsp of rock salt
- **Few sprigs of coriander,** cut coarsely

Wash and cut all the above vegetables into small pieces and add them to a big bowl, mixing them nicely. Food processors can also be used to cut these

Other ingredients

- 100 g of besan (gram flour)
- 1 tsp of rock salt, more can be added as per taste
- ½ tsp of haldi (turmeric powder)
- 1 tsp of jeera (cumin seeds)
- ¼ tsp of ajwain seeds (carom seeds)
- 1 tbsp of dry methi
- 1 tbsp of yogurt
- 1 tsp of lemon juice
- ½ tsp of baking powder (optional). This makes pakoras crisp
- 150 ml of water (can vary depending on the consistency required)
- **Oil** for frying as required – use **any neutral-flavoured oil** with a high smoking point to deep fry, such as **sunflower oil**

Making batter

1. Add besan, salt, haldi, jeera, ajwain seeds, methi, yogurt and lemon juice to the bowl of cut vegetables and mix them completely.
2. Add water slowly, little, by little and make into a medium consistency. This should neither be too thick nor too thin.
3. Taste the batter and add more salt if required.

Deep fry

1. Take a deep kadai or pan and keep it on medium heat. The quantity of oil should be enough so that pakoras are immersed completely.
2. Drop a small portion of the batter into the oil to see if the oil is hot enough. If the batter rises immediately without browning, it is the right temperature.
3. Make a small ball of the mixture and gently drop it in the hot oil. The number of balls that can be added at any one time will depend on the size of the kadai and the quantity of oil. Do not crowd too many of them as they will get stuck and won't fry well.
4. Do not stir for a few seconds, then start stirring so that they do not stick together. A fork can be used to separate them.
5. When one side of the pakoras firm up, looks cooked and are light brown, turn them over gently and fry the other side.
6. Turn them over a couple of times and fry until crisp and golden.
7. Once done, remove them with a slotted spoon, draining as much oil as possible in the pan.
8. Place these on kitchen paper or in a steel colander.

SAVOURY SNACKS

9. Repeat making the next batches as above. Ensure the oil is not too hot at any time. Heat can be reduced a little anytime to keep the oil at the right temperature.
10. Serve these with any green or imli chutney and a cup of tea or coffee, and enjoy.

Special Note

1. Pakoras make for an excellent evening tea-time snack. These are served with green chutney, yogurt or imli chutney.

SAVOURY SNACKS

COURGETTE PAKORAS

Preparation time: 10 minutes   Cooking time: 20 minutes   Total time: 30 minutes   Serves: 4

Ingredients

- **2 medium-sized courgettes,** cut into thin round pieces (not too thin)
- **100 g of besan (gram flour)**
- **1″ ginger,** grated
- **½ tsp of rock salt** (or as required)
- **⅛ tsp of turmeric powder**
- **¼ tsp of red chilli flakes** (optional)
- **1 green chilli,** crushed finely (optional)
- **1 tsp of dry methi**
- **¼ tsp of ajwain seeds (carom seeds)**
- **½ tsp of baking powder** (optional). This makes pakoras crisp
- **150 ml of water** (can vary depending on the consistency required)
- **Oil** for frying as required. Use **any neutral-flavoured oil** with a high smoking point to deep fry, such as **sunflower oil**

Making batter

1. Take a medium-sized bowl. Add courgettes and sprinkle a little salt, a pinch of chilli powder and keep aside.
2. Take another medium-sized bowl, add gram flour, ginger, salt, turmeric powder, red and green chilli, methi, ajwain seeds and baking powder, and mix these nicely.
3. Add water slowly, little by little, and make into a medium consistency. It should neither be too thick nor too thin.
4. Taste the batter and add more salt if required.

Deep fry

1. Take a deep kadai or pan and keep it on medium heat. The quantity of the oil should be enough so that courgette pieces are immersed completely.
2. While the oil heats, drain all the water from the courgette completely.
3. Drop a small portion of the batter into the oil to see if the oil is hot enough. If the batter rises immediately without browning, it is the right temperature.
4. Dip each slice of courgette in the batter and coat them completely before gently sliding them into the oil. The number of these pieces added at one time will depend on the size of the kadai and the quantity of oil. Do not stir for a few seconds, then start stirring so that they do not stick together.
5. When one side of the pakoras firm up, looks cooked and are light brown, turn them over gently and fry the other side.
6. Turn them over a couple of times and fry until crisp and golden.
7. Once done, remove them with a slotted spoon, draining as much oil as possible in the pan.
8. Place these on kitchen paper or in a steel colander.
9. Repeat making the next batches as above. Ensure the oil is not too hot at any time. Heat can be reduced a little anytime to keep the oil at the right temperature.
10. Serve these with any green or imli chutney and a cup of tea or coffee, and enjoy.

Special Note

1. Pakoras make for an excellent evening tea-time snack. These are served with green chutney, yogurt or imli chutney.

SAVOURY SNACKS

SAVOURY SNACKS

HANDWA

Preparation time: 15 minutes   Cooking time: 40 minutes   Total time: 55 minutes   Serves: 4 to 6

Ingredients

½ cup of ground rice flour
½ cup of yellow lentil flour
1 cup of yogurt
1 carrot, grated or cut into small pieces
1 courgette, grated or cut into small pieces (any other vegetable such as gourd or cabbage can be substituted if preferred)
½ cup of peas
½ tsp of thinly cut pieces of unwaxed lemon
1 tbsp of finely grated ginger
1 green chilli, cut into small pieces (optional)
¼ tsp of red chilli flakes (optional)
¾ tsp of turmeric powder
1½ tsp of rock salt
1 tbsp of lemon juice
1 tbsp of ghee (any other oil can be substituted)
3 tbsp of sesame seeds
¾ tsp of Eno powder
Little warm water if required

Method

Overnight Preparation
Take a big bowl. Add rice flour, yellow lentil flour and yogurt. Mix them thoroughly and keep it in room temperature overnight.

Next Day
1. Preheat the oven to 220°C fan oven.
2. Add all the items in a bowl except sesame seeds and Eno powder. Mix these completely. The mixture should be of the consistency of yogurt. In case the mixture seems thick, a little water can be added.
3. Take a steel plate having 1 to 1½" sides or use a baking tray and grease it with ghee.
4. Sprinkle sesame seeds on the plate.
5. Add Eno salt to the mixture, mix it completely and pour it on the plate immediately and sprinkle sesame seeds on the top.
6. Put in the preheated oven for 40 minutes or until the sides become golden brown.
7. Let it cool down for 15 to 20 minutes.
8. The pieces can be cut into 2" pieces or as preferred.

Special Notes

1. Handwa can be eaten with green chutney, yogurt or imli chutney.
2. Handwa can be eaten as a snack or light lunch.

SAVOURY SNACKS

BESAN PUDA

| Preparation time: 25 minutes | Cooking time: 15 minutes | Total time: 40 minutes | Makes: 6 to 7 pudas |

INGREDIENTS

175 g of besan (gram flour)
1 small onion, cut into small pieces
1″ ginger, grated
¼ unwaxed lemon, grated
¾ tsp of rock salt (or as required)
⅛ tsp of turmeric powder
¼ tsp of red chilli flakes (optional)
1 green chilli, crushed finely (optional)
1 tsp of dry methi
Few sprigs of coriander, cut coarsely
¼ tsp of ajwain seeds (carom seeds)
1 tbsp of olive oil
1 tbsp of sesame seeds
150 to 200 ml of water (can vary depending on the consistency required)
Oil for frying, as needed

METHOD

1. Add gram flour to a large mixing bowl.
2. Add all the other ingredients – onion, ginger, lemon, salt, turmeric powder, flaked chilli, green chilli, methi, coriander, ajwain seeds and oil to the bowl. Mix well until combined nicely.
3. Slowly add water, whisking all the time to make a smooth, lump-free batter.
4. Before cooking, allow the besan mixture to rest for 10 minutes.
5. Keep the frying pan on medium heat. You can use a heavy-based steel frying pan. Add ½ to 1 tbsp of oil to grease it nicely. When it gets hot, add 1 big serving spoonful of besan mixture to the pan and spread it around.
6. Cook it on medium-low heat until the bubbles cover the puda, about 1 to 2 minutes.
7. Gently run a spatula, preferably steel, under the puda slowly and make sure it is not stuck to the pan and then flip it over. Make sure not to flip it over too soon as it may break. The puda needs to become a little bit stronger before it is flipped over.
8. Cook until both sides have turned slightly brown. Remove from the pan. Repeat until all the batter is used.
9. Enjoy them while these are hot.

SPECIAL NOTES

1. Besan pudas can be served with yogurt raita or any other type of chutney.
2. Besan puda can be eaten as breakfast along with meetha puda or enjoyed as a snack also. This is one of the popular North Indian dishes.

SAVOURY SNACKS

CHEESY CREPES

| Preparation time: 20 minutes | Cooking time: 25 minutes | Total time: 45 minutes | Makes: 12 crepes |

Ingredients

For crepes

125 g of plain flour
2 g of rock salt
250 ml of milk
3 eggs
2 tbsp of melted butter
Some extra butter or oil for frying

For filling

100 g of grated mozzarella cheese (any other cheese of your choice can be used)
2 medium-sized onions, cut into small pieces
2 medium-sized tomatoes, cut into small pieces
1 green chilli, cut into small pieces (optional)
½ tsp of red chilli flakes (optional)
¾ tsp of rock salt
½ tsp of finely ground pepper
Few sprigs of coriander, cut coarsely

Method

1. Take a big bowl, add flour and salt, and combine nicely. Keep aside.
2. Beat the eggs, whisk them lightly and add to the milk. Add butter and combine these nicely.
3. Add half of this mixture to the flour and set the other half aside.
4. Cover it and set it aside for approximately an hour.
5. After 1 hour, the other half of the milk mixture should also be mixed with the flour mixture. Both of these should be combined properly so that there are no visible lumps. Crepes will come out better if left for an hour.
6. Take a heavy-based pan, preferably steel, and keep it on high/medium heat. Once it gets hot, add a few drops of butter or oil and spread it nicely.
7. Take one serving spoon filled with batter, spread it onto the pan and swirl it so that the batter evenly covers the bottom. The batter can also be flattened with the back of the spoon. In about a minute or so, when the edges of the crepe start to pull away, flip it over using a steel spatula. Cook for another 30 seconds or until it has changed colour to little pink and transfer to a plate. Repeat this process, stacking the crepes on top of each other until the whole batter is finished. You will get about 12 crepes. Leave these to cool.
8. Make the filling by adding cheese, onion, tomato, green chilli, red chilli, salt, pepper and coriander in a bowl. Combine these properly.
9. Take 1 crepe and place it on a plate. Then take 2 tbsp of the cheese mixture and spread it on the centre of the crepe and fold it into a round shape and transfer to a tray. Continue making the rounds with all the crepes until all the crepes are finished. Cut the crepes in half and transfer them to a tray.
10. Preheat the oven to 220°C and keep the tray in the oven for 7 to 8 minutes or until the sides start getting a little brown.
11. Enjoy the crepes straight from the oven while they are hot with green mango chutney.

SAVOURY SNACKS

SAVOURY SNACKS

PAPDI CHAAT

This North Indian street food is everyone's favourite. This sweet, spicy and tangy recipe can be easily made at home, and it is super easy to make.

Preparation time: 25 minutes   Total time: 25 minutes   Serves: 4

Ingredients

Dry ingredients
20 to 25 pieces of papdi
¼ cup of thin sev

Wet ingredients
½ **cup of potatoes,** boiled and cut into small cubes
½ **cup of boiled chickpeas**
2 **tbsp of onions,** cut into tiny pieces
1 **green chilli, cut** into tiny pieces (optional)
2 **tbsp of fresh coriander,** coarsely cut in small pieces, half of which should be kept aside for decoration
2 **tbsp of pomegranate seeds** for decoration

Spices
½ **tsp of Himalayan sea salt,** more can be added after tasting and as per your preference
¼ **tsp of roasted cumin powder**
¼ **tsp of red chilli flakes** (optional)
½ **tsp of chat masala**

Accompaniments
1 **cup of yogurt,** nicely whisked
2 **tbsp of tamarind (Imli) chutney**
2 **tbsp of green chutney**

Method
1. Spread papdis on a big, flat platter.
2. Then top these with potatoes, chickpeas and onions.
3. Add yogurt on top all over. As per your liking, you can put as much as you like.
4. Now sprinkle with salt, cumin powder, chilli powder and chat masala.
5. Followed by green chutney.
6. And then the tamarind chutney. You can adjust the amount of chutney as per your preference.
7. Finish the papdi chaat with pomegranate seeds, sev and coriander.
8. Serve immediately as its crispiness can only be maintained if eaten as soon as it is prepared.
9. It is always preferred to keep some extra chutneys and spices at the side in case anyone prefers to add more of these.

Advance preparations

Papdi chaat is very easy to assemble, but it requires preparing in advance.
1. Potatoes can be boiled 1 or 2 days in advance.
2. Chickpeas can also be boiled a day in advance.
3. Chutneys can be made in advance. You can refer to the category chutneys and raita for these. Tamarind chutney can be made in advance and can be kept in the fridge for up to a month. Green chutney can be kept in the fridge for up to a week.

SAVOURY SNACKS

4. For shortcuts, a few ingredients can easily be bought from Indian stores, such as papdi, tamarind chutney and boiled chickpeas cans.

Special Notes

1. Papdi chaat should be prepared and eaten immediately, as it will become soggy if left for some time.
2. To make it **vegan**, plant-based yogurt can be used.

SAVOURY SNACKS

HEALTHY AND NUTRITIOUS ROASTED MAKHANA, MOONG PHALI, SUNFLOWER AND PUMPKIN SEEDS AND MIXED DRY FRUIT

These roasted snacks are delightfully crunchy, healthy, nutritious and tasty that they will have the whole family coming back for more and more. I have added 4 different snacks below. You can make 1 or more as per your preference.

Roasted Sunflower and Pumpkin Seeds

Preparation time: 2 minutes   Cooking time: 15 minutes   Total time: 17 minutes

Ingredients

For the first mixing

- **1 cup of sunflower seeds (80 g)**
- **1 cup of pumpkin seeds (80 g)**
- **1 tbsp of water**
- **½ tsp of Himalayan sea salt or any salt**

For the second mixing

- **½ tbsp of virgin olive oil**
- **½ tsp of amchoor (dry mango powder)**
- **½ tsp of black pepper**
- **¼ tsp of red chilli flakes** (optional)

Method

1. Preheat the oven to 170°C
2. Take a mixing bowl and add both seeds and mix them. Keep it aside.
3. Take a small bowl. Add water and salt, and mix nicely.
4. Mix the salt mixture with the seed mixture.
5. Line the baking tray, then spread the seeds evenly with a spoon and keep them in the preheated oven.
6. Keep it uncovered for 10 minutes, turning once or twice with a spatula. These should have roasted slightly by now.
7. Take it out from the oven, and mix the second mix ingredients with the salted seeds completely.
8. Keep it in the oven for another 5 minutes.
9. Remove from the oven and allow to cool before transferring to an airtight container.

Special Notes

1. Roasted seeds should be ready to be enjoyed at any time of the day as a snack and will give you energy.
2. Roasted seeds can remain good for a month if kept in an airtight container.

Roasted Peanuts

These roasted peanuts are a convenient snack to take when going for walks, road trips, hiking adventures or days at the beach. This recipe is very easy to make.

| Preparation time: 2 minutes | Cooking time: 30 minutes | Total time: 32 minutes |

Ingredients

For the first mixing

400 g of shelled peanuts
2 tbsp of water
¾ tsp of Himalayan sea salt

For the second mixing

2 tbsp of extra virgin olive oil
¾ tsp of amchoor (mango powder)
½ tsp of black pepper
½ tsp of red chilli flakes

Method

1. Preheat the oven to 150°C.
2. Take a medium-sized bowl and add the ingredients of the first mixing. Mix these completely.
3. Take a shallow baking tray, add the peanuts to the tray and spread them evenly.
4. Keep it uncovered for 15 minutes.
5. Take it out and mix it with spatula and put it back in for another 10 minutes.
6. After 10 minutes, take the peanuts out and mix all the ingredients that are in the second mixing.
7. Keep the tray in the oven for another 5 minutes or until they are golden brown in colour.
8. Take these out of the oven and let them cool. These will continue cooking until they cool down.
9. Once they cool down, these should be transferred to an airtight container.

Special Note

1. Roasted peanuts can remain good for a month if kept in an airtight container.

SAVOURY SNACKS

Roasted Makhana (Fox Nuts)

Roasted makhana is a healthy snack that is made by slow roasting with dry seasonings and herbs.

Preparation time: 2 minutes Cooking time: 10 minutes Total time: 12 minutes

Ingredients

60 g of raw makhanas
1 tsp of ghee or olive oil
¼ tsp of turmeric/haldi
¼ tsp of red chilli flakes
½ tsp of amchoor/mango powder
½ tsp of Himalayan sea salt
½ tsp of chat masala

Method

1. Take a heavy-based pan and keep it on low heat.
2. Add ghee or oil, and as soon as it becomes a little hot, add makhanas and continue stirring it for 8 to 10 minutes or until they become crisp.
3. Then add all the spices except chat masala and mix them well.
4. Turn off the heat so that the spices are not burnt.
5. Lastly, add the chat masala and again mix these well.
6. These roasted makhanas are ready to serve as soon as they become lukewarm or cool to room temperature.
7. Once these cool down, store them in an airtight container.

Special Note

1. You can change the recipe by adding your favourite seasonings and spices, but these should be only dry spices or herbs.

SWEET SNACKS

SWEET SNACKS

FLAPJACK

| Preparation time: 10 minutes | Cooking time: 30 minutes | Total time: 40 minutes | Makes: 20 flapjacks |

Ingredients

140 g of organic jumbo oats
20 g of desiccated coconut
50 g of finely ground pumpkin seeds
20 g of finely ground sunflower seeds
50 g of light brown sugar
1 tbsp of golden syrup
100 g of butter, plus a little extra to grease the baking tray
15 g of sesame seeds

Method

1. Preheat the oven to 160°C.
2. Add oats, desiccated coconut, pumpkin and sunflower seeds in a big bowl.
3. Place a medium pan on medium heat and add butter. Leave it to melt. Add sugar and golden syrup and continue stirring continuously until these are mixed properly. There is no need to boil.
4. Bring the pan off the heat and pour the butter mixture onto the oats making sure that all the oats are covered completely. Combine these nicely.
5. Grease the baking tray and sprinkle half of the sesame seeds on the tray. Then pour the oat mixture onto the plate. Make sure that the oat mixture is spread evenly. This can be levelled evenly using a big spoon, or a small flat steel bowl can also be used to level it down evenly.
6. Sprinkle the remaining sesame seeds over the top.
7. Bake for 30 minutes in the preheated oven or until brown on the sides.

8. Remove from the oven and leave it to cool for 8 to 10 minutes.
9. Cut the flapjack into pieces of 20 or less as required.

Special Note

1. Instead of sugar, try using isomaltulose, a natural alternative to sugar that contains far fewer calories than sugar and thus can have great benefits for those concerned about blood sugar levels. Moreover, the glycemic index (GI) of isomaltulose is much lower than it is for sugar.

SWEET SNACKS

ALMOND BISCUITS

| Preparation time: 20 minutes | Cooking time: 15 minutes | Total time: 35 minutes | Makes: 10 biscuits |

Dry ingredients

350 g of almond flour
70 g of sugar
¼ tsp of sea salt
2 tsp of baking powder
25 g of hazelnuts, broken into pieces (optional)

Wet ingredients

70 g of butter, measured solid, then melted; **can use ghee or coconut oil** for dairy-free
2 large eggs

Method

1. Preheat the oven to 180°C/350°F.
2. Line a baking tray with parchment paper.
3. Mix the dry ingredients together in a large bowl. Stir in the wet ingredients. Form into a dough.
4. Scoop tablespoons of the dough onto the lined baking sheet (a cookie scoop is the fastest way). If it does not work well, small rounds can be made with your hands. A little butter or ghee is required to put on your palm, and rounds can be made. These can then be flattened slightly with your fingers to form into biscuit shapes.
5. Bake for about 15 minutes, until firm and golden. Cool on the baking sheet.

Special Notes

1. These biscuits are favourites of our grandchildren.
2. Instead of sugar, try using isomaltulose, a natural alternative to sugar that contains far fewer calories than sugar and thus can have great benefits for those concerned about blood sugar levels. Moreover, the glycemic index (GI) of isomaltulose is much lower than it is for sugar.

SWEET SNACKS

SWEET & SALTY PEANUT BUTTER ROUNDIES

| Preparation time: 45 minutes | Cooking time: 15 minutes | Total time: 60 minutes | Makes: 35 roundies |

Ingredients

114 g of unsalted butter, softened at room temperature
75 g of sugar
85 g of light brown sugar
205 g of unsweetened peanut butter chunky (creamy can be used if preferred)
1 egg
125 g of millet flour (all-purpose flour can be used if preferred)
¼ tsp of rock salt
Flaky sea salt and coarse sugar for sprinkling

Method

1. Preheat the oven to 180°C/350°F. Line a baking tray with parchment paper or non-stick liners.
2. In a big bowl, add butter and sugars and mix with an electric mixer until smooth and fluffy, for at least 3 minutes. Add the peanut butter and egg, and mix again.
3. Add the flour and salt and mix until well combined. No white flour should be seen.
4. Take a big oven tray and spread the baking sheet on it.
5. Take 1 tbsp of dough and make a round in the palm of your hand and place it on to the sheet. Continue making others and keep placing them on the same tray.
6. These cookies should be flattened with the tip of the finger. These roundies will not spread much or change shape, so they can be placed quite close together, leaving little room between them.
7. In a small bowl, mix 1 tbsp of sugar and ¼ tbsp of salt. Sprinkle each roundie lightly with this mixture.
8. Bake for 12 to 15 minutes until they change to golden brown colour. Carefully lift or slide off the baking sheets and cool on racks, or this can be moved gently and left on the sheet for some time.
9. Store in layers separated by parchment paper, in airtight containers.

Special Notes

1. I use millet flour instead of all-purpose flour as it is diabetic-friendly.
2. These biscuits are favourites of grandparents and their grandchildren.
3. Instead of sugar, try using isomaltulose, a natural alternative to sugar that contains far fewer calories than sugar and thus can have great benefits for those concerned about blood sugar levels. Moreover, the glycemic index (GI) of isomaltulose is much lower than it is for sugar.

SWEET SNACKS

SWEET SNACKS

COCONUT FLOUR COOKIES

Preparation time: 10 minutes   Cooking time: 10 minutes   Total time: 20 minutes   Makes: 25 cookies

Dry ingredients

100 g of coconut flour / ¾ cup
1½ tsp of baking powder
¼ tsp of sea salt
6 tbsp of butter
12 tbsp of coconut oil / ⅓ cup
1 tbsp of sugar
4 large eggs
1 tbsp of almond milk
1 tsp of vanilla extract

Method

1. Preheat the oven to 190°C/375°F.
2. Line a baking tray with parchment paper.
3. Stir together coconut flour, baking soda and salt in a large bowl.
4. In a separate bowl, beat butter and coconut oil together. Add sugar and beat until fluffy.
5. Add eggs, almond milk and vanilla and beat nicely.
6. Add dry ingredients to the wet mixture, beating until mixed nicely. The batter should be thick. If not, add a bit more coconut flour. Be careful not to overdo it.
7. Scoop tablespoons of dough onto the baking sheet and flatten them out to desired thickness.
8. Bake for 8 to 10 minutes or until edges start to brown.

Special Notes

1. These biscuits are favourites of grandparents for their grandchildren.
2. Instead of sugar, try using isomaltulose, a natural alternative to sugar that contains far fewer calories than sugar and thus can have great benefits for those concerned about blood sugar levels. Moreover, the glycemic index (GI) of isomaltulose is much lower than it is for sugar.

DESSERTS

DESSERTS

PANEER DEE KHEER

Preparation time: 5 minutes   Cooking time: 15 minutes   Total time: 20 minutes   Serves: 4

Ingredients

500 ml of full-fat whole milk
¼ tsp of cardamom powder
100 g of paneer, grated
1 tbsp of milk powder
30 g of sugar
1 tbsp of almond powder
½ tbsp of flaxseed powder
2 tbsp of flaked almonds, roasted
1 tbsp of pistachios, chopped or sliced
5 to 6 strands of saffron (optional)

Method

1. Take a wide-bottomed, heavy pan, add milk, and keep it on medium heat. Bring the milk to a boil. As soon as it starts boiling, add cardamom powder and let it boil for 3 to 5 minutes, reducing the heat to low.
2. Add paneer and milk powder to the milk, mix them well and bring it to a boil. As soon as it starts boiling, reduce the heat to low and leave it on the heat for another 5 minutes. This needs to be stirred a couple of times to avoid sticking to the base.
3. Add sugar, almond powder and flaxseed powder and leave it on heat for another 5 minutes.
4. Garnish the kheer with flaked almonds and pistachios, and at the end, add a few strands of saffron.
5. Saffron strands should be mixed with 1 to 2 tbsp of milk, then added at the same time when adding nuts and sugar.

Special Notes

1. Kheer can be eaten hot, warm or chilled.
2. This is a quick, easy and delicious recipe.
3. Instead of sugar, try using isomaltulose, a natural alternative to sugar that contains far fewer calories than sugar and thus can have great benefits for those concerned about blood sugar levels. Moreover, the glycemic index (GI) of isomaltulose is much lower than it is for sugar.

DESSERTS

CHIA PUDDING

Preparation time: 10 minutes   Total time: 10 minutes   Serves: 4

Ingredients

400 ml of coconut milk
45 g of chia seeds
1 tbsp of sugar
½ tsp vanilla extract
Some additional coconut milk for serving
Some fresh or frozen berries for serving

Method

1. Add coconut milk, chia seeds, sugar and vanilla extract in a bowl or in a jar and combine them nicely. Coconut milk should be mixed well so that no lumps are left.
2. Cover it and keep it in the fridge overnight or for at least 4 hours.
3. Serve the pudding with some additional coconut milk and berries.

Special Notes

1. This is a quick, easy and delicious recipe.
2. To give a different flavour to this pudding, cinnamon, cardamom or unsweetened cocoa powder can be added.
3. Instead of sugar, try using isomaltulose, a natural alternative to sugar that contains far fewer calories than sugar and thus can have great benefits for those concerned about blood sugar levels. Moreover, the glycemic index (GI) of isomaltulose is much lower than it is for sugar.

DESSERTS

RICE KHEER FROM MALABAR

| Preparation time: 5 minutes | Cooking time: 40 minutes | Total time: 45 minutes | Serves: 5 to 6 |

Ingredients

50 g of basmati rice
2 tbsp of water
1 litre of whole milk
½ tsp of crushed cardamom (Ilaychi)
1 pinch of cinnamon powder (dalchini)
60 g of sugar
40 g of chopped almonds (badam)
20 g of chopped pistachio (pista)
Few strands of saffron (optional)

Method

1. Rinse the rice until the water turns clear. Then soak it in hot water for at least 10 minutes. After 10 minutes, drain the water and set aside.
2. Take a heavy-based pan and add little water in it and keep it on medium/high heat. Add milk, cardamom and cinnamon powder. Keep stirring until it comes to a boil.
3. Add rice and continue stirring until it starts boiling again.
4. Once it starts boiling, lower the heat and let it simmer for 25 minutes, stirring every 2 minutes.
5. The milk will reduce considerably after 25 minutes, and the kheer will look thick. If you want the kheer thicker, cook for another 10 to 15 minutes.
6. Add sugar and mix it well. Add almond and pistachio, leaving a little portion for decoration.
7. Cook the kheer for another 5 minutes after adding sugar and nuts. Make sure that the sugar is completely dissolved. Don't worry if the kheer doesn't look very thick at this point. It will continue to thicken as it cools down.
8. Remove the pan from heat and transfer to a bowl. Decorate with nuts, and at the end, add few strands of saffron.

Special Notes

1. Kheer can be served hot or chilled. If required to be chilled, it should be chilled and then kept in the fridge for 4 to 5 hours.
2. If using saffron, it should be mixed in 1 to 2 tbsp of milk and mixed with the kheer at the same time when adding nuts.
3. Instead of sugar, try using isomaltulose, a natural alternative to sugar that contains far fewer calories than sugar and thus can have great benefits for those concerned about blood sugar levels. Moreover, the glycemic index (GI) of isomaltulose is much lower than it is for sugar.

DESSERTS

DESSERTS

KADA PRASHAD/AATE KA HALWA

What Is Kada Prashad?

Kada prashad or aate ka halwa is a simple recipe. This is mainly used in Sikh gurudwaras/Sikh temples. Kada prashad made in a gurudwara is a blessing in itself and therefore considered divine. This can also be used at home for doing any prayers and afterwards distributed as prashad to the family members.

This can also be made as a dessert with nuts, raisins and cinnamon powder added to it. The kada prashad made in a gurudwara is made without any addition of nuts, etc.

| Preparation time: 5 minutes | Cooking time: 15 minutes | Total time: 20 minutes | Serves: 4 |

Ingredients

For making kada prashad

- ½ **cup of butter**
- ½ **cup of wheat flour**
- 2 **cups of water**
- ½ **cup of sugar**

For making a dessert

All the same ingredients as detailed above are added in addition to these:
- 3 **tbsp of mixed almonds, pistachios and walnut cut into small pieces**
- 1 **tbsp of mixed raisins and goji berries**
- ¼ **tsp of cinnamon powder**

Method

1. Take a pan and add water and sugar to it and keep on medium fire. Go on stirring so that it does not stick to the base of the pan. Once the sugar is completely mixed and it reaches the boiling point, reduce the heat to the lowest setting and keep aside.
2. Take a kadai/frying pan and keep it on medium fire.
3. Add butter to the kadai, and as soon as it melts, add flour and start stirring with a wooden spatula. While stirring, the heat can be increased to high for a minute or so, but better to keep it on medium to avoid the mixture getting burnt or becoming dark brown.
4. As soon as the mixture changes its colour and looks light brown, the heat should be reduced to the lowest point and sugary water should be added slowly. This may take 3 to 5 minutes.
5. As soon as the water is added, it should be stirred quickly while heat is reduced to low.
6. The reason the mixture needs to be stirred quickly is that if not stirred quickly, some coagulations can be generated.

DESSERTS

This mixture will start moving round and round within a few minutes.
7. You should continue stirring until the butter starts oozing out from the sides and the whole mixture is going round and round.
8. At this point, this should be taken out in a bowl and can be used as kada prashad.
9. In case this is to be used as a dessert, the mixture of nuts, raisins and cinnamon powder should be added and stirred for another 2 minutes. A few pieces can be left aside for sprinkling on the top before serving.
10. Serve immediately.

Special Notes

1. It tastes best if eaten while it is still hot.
2. Instead of sugar, try using isomaltulose, a natural alternative to sugar that contains far fewer calories than sugar and thus can have great benefits for those concerned about blood sugar levels. Moreover, the glycemic index (GI) of isomaltulose is much lower than it is for sugar.

DESSERTS

GAJAR DA HALWA

Preparation time: 15 minutes   Cooking time: 30 minutes   Total time: 45 minutes   Serves: 8

Ingredients

1 kg of carrot, washed, peeled and grated
½ tsp of cardamom powder
150 g of sugar
150 g of butter
75 g of dry milk powder
50 g of almonds, cut into small pieces
25 g of pistachios, cut into small pieces

Method

1. Take a heavy-based medium-sized pan and put on medium heat.
2. Add carrots, cardamom powder and sugar. Leave it uncovered so that the water from the carrots dries up.
3. Stir it regularly to avoid sticking to the base. It may take approximately 15 to 20 minutes.
4. As soon as the water from the sugar and carrot dries up, add butter and continue stirring until it changes colour slightly and you can see the butter showing on the sides of the pan.
5. After 10 minutes or as soon as you start seeing little butter on the sides, add milk and continue stirring it.
6. The halwa should be stirred continuously, or else it can easily burn. After stirring for another 5 minutes, add almonds and pistachios, leaving some for decoration, and mix these together for another minute or so.
7. Remaining almond and pistachio pieces can be sprinkled on the top before serving.
8. Halwa can be served hot as a dessert, or this can be turned into barfi and eaten cold.

Special Notes

1. This is one of the special North Indian desserts.
2. If you decide to make it into barfi, take a big steel plate, sprinkle a little ghee on the plate and spread it nicely.
3. Pour the halwa and spread it evenly with the back of a big spoon or a small flat-based steel bowl.
4. Sprinkle the remaining almond and pistachio pieces on the top and press them down a little. Leave it for 15 minutes, then cut it into 1 or 1½" pieces.
5. These can be served immediately, and remaining can be kept in an airtight container in the fridge.
6. These can remain good in the fridge for at least 20 days.
7. Instead of sugar, try using isomaltulose, a natural alternative to sugar that contains far fewer calories than sugar and thus can have great benefits for those concerned about blood sugar levels. Moreover, the glycemic index (GI) of isomaltulose is much lower than it is for sugar.

KEY INGREDIENTS

HOW TO MAKE HOMEMADE GHEE

Ghee is a delicious ingredient, which produces an aromatic smell, and it is considered to be good for health if used in moderation. I use it to make traditional Indian curries and stir-fried vegetables, pancakes, biscuits, etc., and these are fully enjoyed by my family. It is easy to make at home.

Preparation time: 5 minutes   Cooking time: 35 minutes   Total time: 40 minutes

Ingredients

5 packets (250 g) of unsalted organic butter
1 tbsp of wheat flour

Method

1. Take a medium-sized, heavy-based steel pan and place it on medium heat. Open all the packets of butter and add them to the pan. Heat should be kept on medium until the butter is fully melted. It should be occasionally stirred. This process will take approximately 10 to 12 minutes.
2. Add flour to the melted butter and mix it thoroughly.
3. Reduce the heat to low. It is advisable to keep a long steel spoon in the pan at all times as it helps prevent the ghee from spilling over while boiling.
4. The pan should be kept uncovered, or it can be half-covered if preferred. The butter should be continuously stirred every 5 to 7 minutes.
5. After approximately 20 minutes, you will see ghee being separated from the other solids. Solids will start sticking to the base of the pan. The colour of the solids will change to light pink.
6. At this point, ghee is fully prepared.
7. Allow the ghee to cool slightly for 3 to 5 minutes. Line a fine-mesh strainer with kitchen paper or a triple layer of cheesecloth if available. Place the lined strainer over a heatproof container like a glass bottle. Carefully pour the

mixture through the sieve; the pink solids should be collected on the kitchen paper and should be discarded.
8. Once it cools completely, it will become opaque and light yellow.
9. You can store the ghee at room temperature in a cupboard away from direct light for a few months. If you plan to keep it longer, it is best to store it in the refrigerator.

Special Notes

1. Ghee is a traditional Indian food and has been enjoyed in the Middle East and Asia for thousands of years. It is also frequently used in Ayurveda and other healing medicines.
2. I use flour as it helps the milk solids to be separated from ghee and helps them to settle down at the base so the liquid ghee can easily be drained out.

KEY INGREDIENTS

HOW TO MAKE HOMEMADE YOGURT

Homemade yogurt is healthy and easy to make. This is my preferred method for perfect, thick yogurt every time.

Time: whatever it takes to boil the milk

INGREDIENTS

1 litre of organic whole milk
1 tbsp of yogurt kept from the previous homemade yogurt

METHOD

1. Take a medium heavy-based pan and keep it on medium heat. Add the milk to the pan and bring it to a boil.
2. Leave the milk to cool down until it becomes lukewarm.
3. When the milk becomes lukewarm, it is ready for making yogurt.
4. The milk should be transferred from 1 pan to the other a couple of times. This process helps in making thicker yogurt. Once this process is complete, the milk should be returned to a medium-sized bowl.
5. Add the yogurt to the lukewarm milk and mix it thoroughly.
6. Cover the bowl and keep it in a warm place.
7. I use a small blanket and a towel to keep the bowl warm and place it in a warm area. The best place is the boiler room.
8. Spread the blanket on the shelf or the area where the yogurt is to be kept. The bowl should be kept in the middle of the blanket, and then the towel should be wrapped around the bowl. Finally, the wrapped bowl of milk should be covered from all sides with the blanket so that no air can come inside. Some heavy item should be kept on the top so that the bowl is not moved.

9. It should not be touched or opened for 7 to 8 hours. The best time is to keep it overnight.
10. At this point, the thick, yummy yogurt should be ready to eat.

SPECIAL NOTE

1. Yogurt is 'extremely versatile' and can be used in countless ways in the kitchen. It can be eaten plain, used as dips, raitas, dessert, for making smoothies or even eaten for breakfast with cereal and fruit.

KEY INGREDIENTS

INDIAN MASALA CHAI (SPICED MILK TEA)

What makes an authentic Masala Chai is the use of freshly ground whole spices, which are easily available at home. For many people, it is a perfect way to kick-start the day.

| Masala preparation time: 5 minutes | Tea preparation time: 10 minutes | Total time: 15 minutes |

INGREDIENTS FOR MAKING MASALA

25 green cardamom
2″ of cinnamon stick
1 spoon of fennel seeds (optional)
Grated ginger as per taste
Little milk. The quantity of milk depends upon your liking
The above masala will be enough to make approximately 20 cups

METHOD

Mix cardamom and cinnamon, grind them in a grinder or food processor, and keep in a jar. Separately, fennel seeds can be ground and kept in a separate jar. This is optional.

METHOD OF MAKING MASALA TEA

1. Add 2 cups of water to a pan. Add ½ tsp of the mixture of cardamom and cinnamon, ¼ tsp of fennel seed powder, a little ginger and bring it to a boil. These ingredients can be increased or decreased as preferred. Once the water starts boiling, let it simmer for 1 to 2 minutes. Now, the water is ready to make tea.
2. Add ½ tsp of tea leaves per cup in the water and bring it to a simmer for another ½ minute. The time to boil the water after the tea is added depends upon the way you want to have it. If you prefer strong tea, then you should boil it for a minute but if you want light tea, 30 seconds should be fine.
3. At this point, add a little milk and let it boil for ½ to 1 minute. Once you see the brown colour, you can switch off the heat and drain it into a tea pot or into individual cups.
4. Enjoy the tea with snacks and biscuits.

SPECIAL NOTES

1. Any type of loose tea can be used, though the popular one is a mixture of Darjeeling and Assam tea.
2. The ratio is ⅓ Darjeeling and ⅔ Assam tea.
3. Tea is enjoyed with any type of pakoras such as aloo pakoras, onion pakoras, mixed vegetables pakoras or cauliflower pakoras, and with almonds, coconut biscuits or peanut sandies.
4. All the above snacks are on this site, Renurecipes.com.
5. If you prefer to have black tea, you can still have it following the same method but avoiding adding milk.

KEY INGREDIENTS

KEY INGREDIENTS

INDIAN CURRY MASALA

Basic Indian curry sauce, also called Bhuna masala, is made with onions, garlic, ginger, tomatoes and spices. This is the base for many Indian dishes such as lentils and curries. This masala is very versatile and freezes well. It is perfect for those busy days when you want to make a curry in a hurry.

The term 'masala' refers to a combination of many spices and is common in Indian cooking. It is frequently utilised in the preparation of foods such as soups, stews, lentils, beans and curries as a base. Masala can vary widely based on region and personal preference. It adds flavour and complexity to dishes that would otherwise be bland.

Masala made with the ingredients given below can be used to make 4 or 5 curries, lentils and any other sauce-based recipes for 5 to 6 people.

Ingredients

½ **cup of ghee or oil** of your choice
5 **onions, 12 cloves of garlic, 3″ ginger** cut into tiny pieces or chopped in a food processor
5 **medium-sized fresh tomatoes** chopped **or 1 (400 ml) and a half tin of chopped tomatoes**
2 **tbsp of tomato puree**
4 **green chillies** (optional)

Spices

2½ **tsp of jeera (cumin seeds)**
1 **tsp of black rye (mustard seeds)**
1 **tsp of ground turmeric**
5 **tsp of coriander powder**
1 **tsp of red chilli flakes** (optional)

Method

1. To make masala, add ghee or oil to a medium-sized pan. As soon as it becomes a little hot, add jeera and rye seeds. When they start bubbling, add the onion mixture. Reduce the heat and let it cook for 5 to 6 minutes or until it turns pinkish.
2. Add turmeric, coriander powder and chilli and mix it completely.
3. Soon after, add chopped tomatoes, tomato puree and green chilli, and mix these again.
4. Cover the pan so that the tomatoes are combined properly and turn into a smooth paste. Leave this covered for another 7 to 8 minutes. This paste should be stirred occasionally so that it does not get burned.
5. The masala is ready when it starts to show a little oil on the sides of the pan.

Special Notes

1. Oil can be used to make the masala **vegan**.
2. This sauce stores well in the refrigerator for up to a week.
3. This masala can be divided into 4 or 5 small plastic boxes, kept in the freezer and used as and when required.
4. The masala remains good in the freezer for 3 to 4 months.

KEY INGREDIENTS

GRANDCHILDREN FAVOURITES

GRANDCHILDREN FAVOURITES

ALOO PURI

Aloo puri is a traditional Punjabi spiced potato curry served with puris. This is also one of the favourite dishes of our grandchildren.

| Preparation time: 25 minutes | Cooking time: 50 minutes | Total time: 75 minutes | Serves: 4 to 5 |

Ingredients

For the aloo sabji

350 g of potatoes or 5 medium-sized potatoes, boiled, peeled and diced, this sabji can also be made with raw potatoes
2 cups of water

Masala or tadka

2 tbsp of ghee or any oil as per your choice
1 tsp of cumin seeds
1 pinch of asafoetida (hing)
½ tsp of black mustard seeds
4 cloves of garlic and 1½″ ginger, chopped in a food processor or cut into tiny pieces
¾ tsp of turmeric powder
1 tsp of coriander powder
1 tbsp of dry fenugreek leaves (methi)
1 tsp of rock salt, more can be added after tasting
½″ of lemon rind, nicely grated
1 tsp of lemon juice
2 tsp of tomato puree
½ a can of chopped tomatoes, approximately 250 g or 2 medium-sized tomatoes chopped in a food processor
1 green chilli, chopped or cut into small pieces (optional)
1 tsp of garam masala
Few sprigs of fresh coriander cut into small pieces, coarsely

Method

If raw potatoes are used, then a pressure cooker can be used. It will require 2 to 3 whistles or more until the potatoes are done.

1. Take a large heavy-bottom pan, keep on medium heat and add ghee or oil of your choice. When the ghee gets a little hot, add asafoetida, cumin and mustard seeds.
2. As soon as it starts bubbling, add the mixture of ginger and garlic and cook them for 1 to 2 minutes, stirring often.
3. Once the colour changes to light pink, add turmeric, coriander powder, fenugreek leaves and salt. After a couple of minutes, add lemon rind, lemon juice, tomato puree, chopped tomato and chilli and mix these nicely.
4. At this point, reduce the heat to low and cover the pan so that the tomatoes are combined properly and turn into a smooth paste. This takes 7 to 8 minutes. This paste should be stirred occasionally so that it does not get burnt.
5. Now add the potatoes and mix them nicely. Soon after, add water and mix it properly, bringing it to a boil.
6. Once it starts boiling, reduce the heat and let it simmer for 8 to 10 minutes.
7. While it is simmering, press a couple of potatoes with the spoon on the sides of the pan.
8. This is to get a slightly thicker consistency of the gravy. Starch from the potatoes also makes the gravy a little thick.
9. Once done, take it out in a serving bowl, sprinkle some garam masala and put the lid on to retain the aroma.
10. Sprinkle fresh coriander before serving.

Ingredients

For the puri

2½ to 3 cups of whole meal flour
1 tsp of oil
Lukewarm water to knead the flour – as required
Oil for frying

Method

1. Knead the flour into a stiff dough with water and oil. The dough for puris needs to be harder than for making chapatis. Once the dough is formed, drizzle with a dash of oil and use your fingers to cover the dough with it. Cover it and keep aside for about 30 minutes.
2. Make small balls of the dough according to your preferred size and shape them into balls. Dredge the working surface and the belan with a splash of oil.
3. Roll into rounds having 4 to 5 inches in diameter. You can roll 5 or more and keep these ready. Use oil instead of flour to roll out the puris as the dry flour will make the frying oil dirty.
4. Heat oil in a kadai or any deep pan at a high temperature. To check if the oil is ready for frying, drop a little piece the size of a pea into the oil and if it comes up immediately, the oil is ready.
5. Start adding puris slowly, 1 puri at a time, and flip each as it puffs up. This should be slightly pressed down with a stainless steel skimmer spatula.
6. When pressed, it puffs up a little. This should be turned over as soon as the colour changes to light brown. It will take only a few seconds.
7. Follow the same process until all the rolled puris are finished. Continue following the same process until the dough is finished.
8. Fry the puris at a high temperature in extra oil for the best, airy puris that don't absorb any extra oil.
9. Puris are ready when they are fully puffed up and are golden brown.
10. Remove and place these on paper napkins to remove excess oil.
11. Serve the puris with aloo sabji, along with sliced onions, some lemon wedges and some pickles.

Makes: 15 to 18 puris

Special Notes

1. Oil can be used to make the recipe **vegan**.
2. You can have the consistency of the aloo sabji as per your preference. However, avoid making it watery or thin. You can always add more water later if you feel the gravy has become too thick.
3. Special care is also taken that potatoes are not too mashed.

GRANDCHILDREN FAVOURITES

GLAZED POPCORN

Preparation time: 5 minutes   Cooking time: 15 minutes   Total time: 20 minutes
Serves: 6 to 8, approximately makes 1 medium-sized bowl

Ingredients

100 g of unpopped popcorn kernels (¾ small cup)
50 g of butter (6 tbsp or half small cup)
25 g of sugar
2 tbsp of sunflower oil or coconut oil
2 tbsp of water

Method

1. Heat the oil in a big saucepan on medium-high heat. If using coconut oil, allow all the solids to melt.
2. As soon as the oil starts visibly vaporising, add popcorn kernels into the pan and cover it with a lid. Wait for 10 to 15 seconds and you will see a couple of popcorn kernels popping. Once these start popping, gently shake the pan by moving it back and forth over the burner. The pan should be continuously moved back and forth until all the kernels have popped.
3. Once the popping slows to several seconds between pops, remove the pan from the heat, remove the lid and transfer the kernels immediately into a wide bowl. With this technique, nearly all the kernels pop and nothing burns. Leave these to cool down.
4. Keep a small pan on medium heat and add butter. As soon as it melts, add sugar. Boil for 2 minutes. Add water and stir well. Quickly pour this over popped corn and toss to coat.
5. Chill the popcorn in the fridge for 15 to 20 minutes before serving.

Special Notes

1. Sweet popcorn is a favourite of grandparents for their grandchildren.
2. Instead of sugar, try using isomaltulose, a natural alternative to sugar that contains far fewer calories than sugar and thus can have great benefits for those concerned about blood sugar levels. Moreover, the glycemic index (GI) of isomaltulose is much lower than it is for sugar.

GRANDCHILDREN FAVOURITES

OAT AND ALMOND PANCAKES

| Preparation time: 10 minutes | Cooking time: 20 minutes | Total time: 30 minutes | Makes: 10 pancakes |

Ingredients

50 g of oat flour
50 g of almond flour
50 g of wholemeal flour
1 pinch of rock salt
2 tsp of light brown sugar (optional)
2 eggs
200 ml of milk
2 tbsp of ghee or butter for frying

Method

1. Combine oat flour, almond flour, wholemeal flour, salt and sugar in a large-sized bowl and keep aside.
2. Beat the eggs slightly and add the milk. Use a wire whisk to whisk the wet ingredients together first before slowly folding them into the dry ingredients. Mix together until smooth (there may be a couple of lumps, but that's okay). Keep the batter aside.
3. Pancakes can be made immediately, but if kept for half an hour or a little more, they may come out a little softer.
4. The batter will be thick and creamy in consistency. If you find the batter too thick and it does not pour off the spoon easily, 1 or 2 extra tbsp of milk can be added until reaching the desired consistency.
5. Heat a pan, preferably a steel one, on a medium/high heat. Once it gets hot, pour ¼ cup or a big serving spoonful of batter onto the pan and spread it into a round shape with the back of the spoon.
6. When the underside is golden and bubbles begin to appear on the surface, flip with a spatula (preferably steel) and cook until both sides turn a golden colour. Repeat the same process with the remaining batter.
7. Serve with agave syrup/honey or lemon and brown sugar or fruit. These can also be enjoyed plain.

Special Note

1. These pancakes are healthy and nutritious and are loved by grandchildren; in fact, these are favourites of the whole family.

GRANDCHILDREN FAVOURITES

PORRIDGE

Preparation time: 5 minutes   Cooking time: 10 minutes   Total time: 15 minutes   Serves: 2

Porridge is one of the favourite breakfast dishes of our grandchildren. For making porridge, I mix 1 cup of jumbo oats, ½ cup of barley flakes and ½ cup of millet flakes, store these in an airtight glass bottle, and use it as and when required.

Ingredients

1 tbsp of butter
100 g of oat mixture
150 ml of water
200 ml of whole milk
Agave syrup or honey
Few strawberries
Few blueberries
Chia seeds, cacao nibs, raisins, chocolate drops or cinnamon powder (optional)

Method

1. Take a heavy-based, medium-sized pan, preferably steel, and keep it on medium heat. As soon as the butter melts, add the oat mixture and combine it nicely, stirring for approximately 1 minute. Make sure that it does not burn.
2. Add water and bring it to a boil. Reduce the heat as soon as it starts boiling and leave it to simmer for 2 minutes. You should ensure that it does not stick to the bottom. You can cover this, but it needs to be stirred continuously.
3. Then add milk and bring the heat to medium and bring it to a boil. As soon as it starts boiling, stir properly and reduce the heat. Cover the pan and continue stirring the mixture continuously, taking care that it does not stick to the bottom.
4. It will take 4 to 5 minutes before it becomes soft and creamy. If the mixture looks thick, a little more milk can be added and stirred while left on low heat.
5. Cold milk can also be added at the time of eating, if it is very hot.
6. This can be eaten with agave syrup or honey. Strawberries and blueberries can also be added to the porridge.
7. Other optional items as listed in the ingredients list can also be added.

Special Note

1. Porridge is a quick and easy-to-prepare recipe. It is a perfect dish to enjoy as it is or to jazz up with your favourite toppings like fruit and spices, or just classic honey. It is one of the best breakfasts to have to maintain a healthy lifestyle.

GRANDCHILDREN FAVOURITES

PASTA WITH FRESH TOMATO SAUCE

| Preparation time: 5 minutes | Cooking time: 25 minutes | Total time: 30 minutes | Serves: 4 |

Pasta with fresh tomato sauce is a favourite lunch or dinner for grandchildren. I am adding this recipe at their request.

Ingredients

8 medium-sized red juicy tomatoes
2 tbsp of water
5 to 6 tbsp of olive oil, half to be used for cooking, the rest for mixing later
1 medium-sized onion, cut into small pieces
3 small garlic cloves, cut into small pieces
¾ tsp of sea salt, more can be added as per taste
½ tsp of dried oregano or mixed herbs
100 g of mature cheddar cheese, grated. Any other hard cheese can be used as per your choice
Few basil or parsley leaves, cut into small pieces
500 g of pasta

Method

1. Wash the tomatoes. Cut them into big pieces. Take a large pan and add the tomatoes to the pan. Add water and keep it on a medium/high heat. Let it boil. As soon as it starts boiling, reduce the heat and let it simmer until the tomatoes become soft. This may take 8 to 10 minutes.
2. Once these are soft, these should be taken out of the water and mashed completely so that no big pieces are visible. Another option is to add the tomato liquid into a food processor and crush them nicely. Keep these aside.
3. Take a medium-sized, heavy-based pan and put on medium heat. Add 2 to 3 tbsp of olive oil, and once it is a little hot, add onion and garlic, stirring for 1 or 2 minutes until they are a little pink. Add mashed or crushed tomato mixture and salt, then increase the heat. Once it starts boiling, add any herb of your choice, such as mixed herbs or oregano, reduce the heat to medium, and leave it to simmer until the sauce has thickened. This may take 12 to 15 minutes.
4. In another big pan, add enough water for boiling the pasta. The heat should be kept on high. Add a little salt and 1 tsp of olive oil. As soon as it starts boiling, add pasta and leave it uncovered on high heat. Keep the pasta a little undercooked or cook it as per the instructions given on the packet.
5. Once cooked, drain the water, keeping half a cup of water that can be used later if required.
6. Add the tomato sauce, half of the cheese, a little black pepper to the boiled pasta and mix these nicely. A few spoons of pasta water can be added if it starts sticking. Add some olive oil.
7. Transfer into a serving bowl, decorate with basil or parsley leaves and serve while it is hot.
8. Some more grated cheese can be added to the pasta before eating.

Special Note

1. To make it **vegan**, any plant-based cheese can be used.

www.ingramcontent.com/pod-product-compliance
Lightning Source LLC
Chambersburg PA
CBRC090746010526
44114CB00008B/99